MESSAGE OF BIBLICAL SPIRITUALITY
Editorial Director: Carolyn Osiek, RSCJ

Volume 1

The Pentateuch

by

Michael D. Guinan, O.F.M.

A Michael Glazier Book
THE LITURGICAL PRESS
Collegeville, Minnesota

ABOUT THE AUTHOR

Michael D. Guinan, O.F.M., studied scripture and semitics at Catholic University of America, receiving his doctorate in 1972. He has taught in the Philippines and in America, and has contributed widely to academic publications.

A Michael Glazier Book
published by
THE LITURGICAL PRESS

Typography by Brenda Belizzone and Phyllis Boyd LeVane.

1   2   3   4   5   6   7   8   9

Library of Congress Cataloging-in-Publication Data
Guinan, Michael D.
    The Pentateuch / by Michael D. Guinan.
        p.   cm. — (Message of biblical spirituality ; v. 1)
    "A Michael Glazier book."
    Includes bibliographical references and indexes.
    ISBN 0-8146-5567-X
    1. Bible. O.T. Pentateuch—Criticism, interpretation, etc.
    2. Spiritual life—Biblical teaching. I. Title. II. Series.
BS1225.2.G85   1990
222'.1106—dc20
                                   90-62042
                                   CIP

EDITOR'S PREFACE

One of the characteristics of church life today is a revived interest in spirituality. There is a growing list of resources in this area, yet the need for more is not exhausted. People are yearning for guidance in living an integrated life of faith in which belief, attitude, affections, prayer, and action form a cohesive unity which gives meaning to their lives.

The biblical tradition is a rich resource for the variety of ways in which people have heard God's call to live a life of faith and fidelity. In each of the biblical books we have a witness to the initiative of God in human history and to the attempts of people not so different from ourselves to respond to the revelation of God's love and care.

The fifteen volumes in the *Message of Biblical Spirituality* series aim to provide ready access to the treasury of biblical faith. Modern social science has made us aware of how the particular way in which one views reality conditions the ways in which one will interpret experience and life itself. Each volume in this series is an attempt to retell and interpret the biblical story from within the faith perspective that originally formed it. Each seeks to portray what it is like to see God, the world, and oneself from a particular point of view and to search for ways to respond faithfully to that vision. We who are citizens of our twentieth century world cannot be people of the ancient biblical world, but we can grow closer to their experience and their faith and thus closer to God, through the living Word of God which is the Bible.

The series includes an international group of authors representing England, Ireland, Canada, and the United States, but whose life experience has included first-hand knowledge of many other countries. All are proven scholars and committed believers whose faith is as important to them as their scholarship. Each acts as interpreter of one part of the biblical tradition in order to enable its spiritual vitality to be passed on to others. It is our hope that through their labor the reader will be able to enter more deeply into the life of faith, hope, and love through a fuller understanding of and appreciation for the biblical Word as handed down to us by God's faithful witnesses, the biblical authors themselves.

Carolyn Osiek, RSCJ
Associate Professor of New Testament Studies
Catholic Theological Union, Chicago

Contents

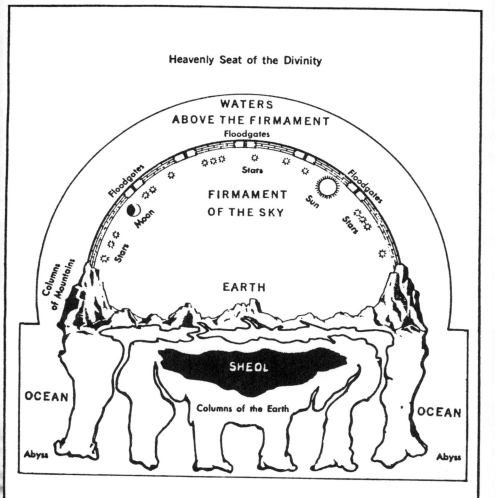

THE WORLD OF THE HEBREWS

THE WORLD OF THE HEBREWS — Graphic representation of the Hebrew conception of the world. God's heavenly seat rests above the superior waters. Below these waters lies the firmament or sky which resembles an overturned bowl and is supported by columns. Through the openings (floodgates) in its vault the superior waters fall down upon the earth in the form of rain or snow. The earth is a platform resting on columns and surrounded by waters, the seas. Underneath the columns lie the inferior waters. In the depths of the earth is Sheol, the home of the dead (also called the nether world). This was the same prescientific concept of the universe as that held by the Hebrews' pagan neighbors.

Dedication

This book is gratefully dedicated to the
students and the faculty of Our Lady of
the Angels Seminary, Quezon City, Philippines

Preface

I remember when I got my first pair of glasses. I could suddenly see things I had either not seen before or had seen but had forgotten—like the edges of leaves or the writing on signs in the distance. This was brought back to me not too long ago when I had to get bifocals. Again I saw things sharply I had not noticed for a while, but this time they were things up close. Whether far off or nearby, our vision sometimes fades, and we need to sharpen things up.

Something similar often happens in our spiritual lives. We go along our usual ways, engaged in our everyday, normal lives; then, without our really noticing, our vision begins to get fuzzy and hazy, and eventually we forget what things looked like. Or we can have new experiences and see new things, but not clearly. And that is too bad because spirituality is above all a question of vision.

How do we *see* God? how do we *see* the world? how do we *see* ourselves as human beings in relation to both God and the world? As religious people in the Judeo-Christian tradition, in order to sharpen our vision, we return to our roots, to our basic story, and try, as it were, to listen to it with new eyes. For the Jewish tradition, that story is found primarily in the Pentateuch (the Torah, the Law of Moses); for the Christian, it is found primarily in the gospel of Jesus Christ. But we Christians too must look at the Pentateuch and take it seriously if we are to understand who Jesus is, for it was precisely to the Pentateuch that the first Christian communities often went, and upon which they drew, as they tried to deepen their awareness and vision of who Jesus was and what he meant.

The earliest Christians who came to follow Jesus were first Jews. They had studied and knew their Torah (Pentateuch) before they had come to know Jesus. In this book, we will, in a way, try to imitate them. We will study the Pentateuch as it is; we will let it speak on its own terms and try not to filter it too much at first through specifically Christian lenses. Far too often, those lenses, smeared with a "Law versus Gospel" brush, have impeded our vision rather than helped it. At times we will allude to New Testament texts, but we will save our discussion of Jesus and the Law until the end. Like the earliest Christians we will attempt to come to Jesus only after we have studied the Torah and have some idea of what it is all about.

The Pentateuch is a large book; of necessity, ours must be a small one. That entails a certain selectivity; certain decisions had to be made about what to include and what to omit (for example, the brief discussion of Leviticus). Inevitably, my own perspective and vision, my own sight and insight intervene. All I can plead is that I have tried to stay close to the text and respect its main contours and emphases.

Needless to say, in doing this I have built on the sights and insights of many others. Rather than clutter the chapters, aimed at a more general readership, with extensive footnotes and the paraphernalia of scholarship, I have chosen to include, at the end of each chapter, some suggestions for further reading which will indicate some of my indebtedness to the work of others. Scholars will no doubt recognize more, which I gratefully acknowledge.

The translation of the biblical text which I use is that of the *New American Bible*. In a few places I have made slight modifications to bring out in English certain nuances and connections, more apparent in the Hebrew, to the issues under discussion. These will be plainly obvious if read along with the NAB text.

The completion of this work took a bit longer than originally anticipated. I would like to thank the editor, Lyn Osiek, for both her patience and her prodding.

Finally, I would like to acknowledge and thank my students and colleagues at Our Lady of the Angels Seminary, Quezon City, Philippines. It was there that I taught a course on the Pentateuch which was, in a way, the first draft of this book, and it was there that a large part of the actual writing took place. I am honored to dedicate this work to them.

Michael D. Guinan, O.F.M.
Franciscan School of Theology
Berkeley, CA 94709

1

The Pentateuch: Introductory Matters

Who am I? Who are we? Where do we come from? How do we fit into the world? In the light of who we are, how are we to live? These are questions of basic, ultimate concern; all religious traditions try, in their various way, to answer them. Within our Judeo-Christian tradition, the answers are found in the sacred writings we call the Bible. For Christians, the primary focus is on the New Testament, especially the first part, the Gospels. For the Jewish community, that primary focus is on the first five books of the Bible, the Pentateuch. Since the New Testament constantly draws on and quotes from the Hebrew Scriptures, it is important also for Christians both to become familiar with and to appreciate these writings.

Title

Pentateuch comes from two Greek words which can be translated roughly as "five scrolls," and refers to the first five books of the Old Testament: Genesis, Exodus, Leviticus, Numbers, and Deuteronomy. While these are now five separate books, each with a certain integrity of its own, they form in fact one continuous story. In Hebrew, it is the overarching unity which is more in focus; these books are known as the *Torah*.

Even though the Hebrew word *torah* properly means "teaching" or "instruction," it has more often, in reference to the Pentateuch, been translated "the Law." Even a cursory reading of the text, however, would show that this is inadequate. While large blocks of legal material do occur, we also meet large blocks of narrative. The *Torah* does give legal material (what Israel must do) but this is squarely within a framework of a story (what God has already done for Israel). Thus, Israel's obeying the law must be seen as a response to God's previous acts. In our last chapter, we will offer a term other than "Law" which may be more helpful in approaching these books.

Content

The Pentateuch tells of the origins of Israel as a people, but begins by setting these events in a wider, even a cosmic, context. *Genesis* opens with a story of the creation of the world and the whole human family. Within this, God's choice falls on one family, that of Abraham, which is called from Mesopotamia to the land of Canaan. He and his descendents, Isaac, Jacob, and Joseph, receive the promise of land, of offspring, and of God's presence. At the end of Genesis, the people have left Canaan because of famine and settled in Egypt.

At the start of *Exodus*, the situation changes dramatically. From comfort and prosperity, the people experience oppression and suffering and call out to God for deliverance. God, now known by the covenant name of Yahweh, calls Moses to lead the people from slavery and into the Sinai desert, there to receive the covenant: "I will be their God, they will be my people." The Tent of Meeting and the Ark of the Covenant are constructed as signs of God's abiding presence.

Leviticus continues the covenant law begun in Exodus and contains many regulations dealing with sacrifices, feasts, the priesthood and obligations of holiness.

Numbers begins with the numbering of the tribes and their organizations as a people on the march. They then wander in the wilderness for forty years as a punishment for rebelling against God and Moses, the chosen leader.

Finally, in *Deuteronomy*, the people are poised across the Jordan River, on the verge of entering the promised land. In three long speeches, Moses recalls God's saving deeds and urges the people to respond to the *Torah* with faithful obedience. After this "farewell discourse," Moses dies.

In summary, the Pentateuch begins with the story of creation and the promises to the ancestors; then follows the oppression in Egypt and the deliverance wrought by Yahweh. It ends with the people wandering in the wilderness until they finally march forward and prepare to enter the land. At its center stands(Mt. Sinai (Ex 19-Nm 10). It is there that the people, under Moses' leadership, enter into covenant with Yahweh and receive the Torah.

The Pentateuch: Product of History

Without doubt, Moses plays a key and pivotal role in the Pentateuch, so much so that later tradition would refer to it simply as "the Law of Moses"; Moses was considered to be its author. Though individual objections to this were raised from earliest times, it is only in the last few centuries that a thorough challenge has been mounted and generally sustained.

First of all, very few texts refer to Moses writing anything (e.g., Ex 17:14; 24:4; 34:27; Nm 33:2; Dt 31:9, 24), and these clearly do not refer to the whole Pentateuch. In addition, some texts could not have been written by Moses, e.g., the account of his own death in Dt 34 and texts with anachronisms of a political and geographical sort. Thus, Gen 21:34 and 26:1 mention the Philistines; the Philistines occupied the southwest coast of Palestine only after the time of Moses; Gen 14:14 refers to the northernmost boundary of the land as "Dan"; the tribe of Dan did not migrate up to that location until long after the death of Moses, as Judges 18 clearly attests. Further, other texts seem to contradict each other. When was Yahweh (translated "the Lord" in most modern versions) first invoked by name, at the time of the ancient ancestors (Gen 4:26; 12:8), or only at the time of the Exodus (Ex 6:2)? How many animals went on the Ark, two of each (Gen 6:19-20) or seven pair of clean animals and only one of unclean (Gen 7:2-3)? How should the paschal lamb be prepared, boiled (Dt 16:7) or not boiled but roasted (Ex 12:9)? These few examples—and there are many more—suffice to point to the problem.

While each of these could be looked at in isolation, it becomes apparent rather quickly that they tend to cluster, to fall together, as it were, into distinct "piles." Scholars generally see four such "piles," each forming a distinct source within the Pentateuch. Two of the sources are primarily narratives which tell the story of Israel's origins; the other two are primarily collections of law. These sources, further, derive from different periods of Israel's history. The oldest dates from the time of the united monarchy (ca. 950 B.C.); the youngest, from the time in or shortly after the Babylonian Exile (587-538 B.C.). This is the so-called "Four Source Theory" which is accepted more or less by mainstream Catholic, Protestant and Jewish scholars today.

The Pentateuch is, then, the end-product of a long process extending over and reflecting much of Israel's history. The figure of Moses and the covenant at Sinai stand as the founding moment of that history. Thus, while Moses may not be the "author" in our modern sense, he can certainly be recognized as the "author-ity" on which Israel's religious identity was based. None of this need upset or compromise a stance of faith that sees in the scriptures the Word of God. It simply points out how this comes to us through the human history and instrumentality of God's people.

The Pentateuch: Source of History

The Pentateuch covers the earliest part of Israel's history; it is, in fact, the main source for our knowledge of this period. The question is: How much historical information does it give us? It was precisely this concern that motivated the scholars of the last two centuries who discerned the four sources.

Some would maintain that the Pentateuch, as written, gives us pure, literal history, a position popularly called "fundamentalist." It is rightly rejected by mainstream Judaism and Christianity; its presupposed views of history and truth are unacceptable, and it fails to deal thoroughly with the data. On the other hand, some are overly skeptical and maintain that we cannot recover any history at all in the Pentateuch.

The truth would seem to lie somewhere in between these two extremes. Historical memories are preserved, but the main purpose of the text is not to present literal history. And when it is concerned with history, it is not concerned to present this as we would today. What kind of history does it present? How and to what extent does archeology help us in our understanding. These are important and complex questions, and they are much debated by scholars.

As important as these historical questions may be, we will not be overly concerned with them in what follows. Our bracketing of them should not be interpreted as taking any particular position in their regard. Without prejudging any historical question, we will prefer to speak of "story" rather than "history." The Pentateuch is a religious document produced, under the guidance of God, by a religious community to answer and deal with religious questions. It is these which will be the focus of our considerations.

✤

Suggested Readings

On the Pentateuch in General, and as the Product of History:

L. Bailey, *The Pentateuch* (Interpreting Biblical Texts; Nashville: Abingdon, 1981) 13-60.

L. Boadt, *ROT*, 89-108.

M. Maher, *Genesis* (OTM 2; 1982) 11-17 (what he presents as an introduction to Genesis applies equally well to the Pentateuch as a whole).

R.E. Murphy, "Introduction to the Pentateuch," *NJBC* #1

On the Pentateuch as Source of History, and on the Role of Archeology:

B. Anderson, *UOT*, 18-27.

L. Boadt, *ROT*, 52-68 (on archeology); 75-80 (on different ways of presenting history; the chart on p. 79 is especially helpful).

J. Maxwell Miller, *The Old Testament and the Historian* (Philadelphia: Fortress Press, 1976).

H. Darrell Lance, *The Old Testament and the Archeologist* (Philadelphia: Fortress Press, 1981).

2

Genesis: Fortunes and Misfortunes of Imagehood

At the beginning of any spirituality lies some conception of God and the human and of their interrelationship. All subsequent beliefs and practices are based on and derive from these. It is precisely this beginning that we find in the book of "beginnings," Genesis, and at the very beginning of this book, in the creation story of chapters 1:1-2:4.

Creation

At the beginning, the world is a disordered chaos, dark, watery, formless and void. In this way, the ancients conceived the pole opposite to the existing world. (Later philosophers and theologians would conceive of this same opposite pole as "nothingness.") Then the creator God begins to subdue the chaos and to call out an ordered universe. This divine activity proceeds through two movements or panels, corresponding to days one-two-three and to days four-five-six.

The action of the first panel is one of separating. On the first day, God separates light from darkness. The power of chaos, of which darkness is a part, begins to recede before the light of the presence of God (see Ps 31:17; 44:4). On the second day, God calls forth a firmament, or dome, which the ancients believed separated the waters above (the source of rain which fell through "floodgates" [Gen 7:11]) from the waters below (the source of seas, springs and fountains). Thus a kind of tent of breathing space emerges. Into this would go the world we know. On the third day, God separates the dry land, the earth, from the water; and from this earth, vegetation of all kinds, plants and trees, comes forth. At the end of the third day, the first panel, God has divided and conquered; the chaos has been subdued. In its place stands a universe with all of its parts in ordered harmony; the stage is set for living beings to appear.

God's action of the second panel is one of filling the spaces of the first panel with beings which move or live in them. On the fourth day (corresponding to the light and darkness of the first day) appear the sources of light, the sun, moon and stars which, through their movement, mark the passage of time and the festal calendar. On the fifth day, the water and air of the second day teem with life, with birds and fishes. These receive a further call to continue God's life-giving activity. On the sixth day, those creatures who live in and off of the earth make their appearance: animals of all kinds and, finally, humans, male and female, who come at the peak of creation and have a special role to play. Finally, on the seventh day, God rests, and all creation shares that rest.

This creation account is beautifully composed and carefully structured. Its general contours, just described, can be diagrammed like this:

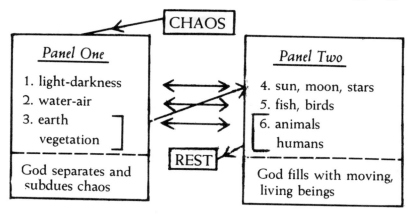

Thus, in the opening verses of Genesis we meet our God, a God who effortlessly, through the power of speech, invites the world into existence. God is the one who has dominion over chaos, who subdues it and brings, in its place, a universe harmonious and habitable, fit for life. God then appears as the source and origin of that life which fills the world. In 2:4a we read, "this is the story" of God's creating. The Hebrew word (*toledoth*) does not literally mean "story," but rather "begettings, geneologies." Everything that is is begotten, derives its life, from the word of God (see Dt 8:3; also Amos 8:11). In a nutshell, this is the meaning of "creation." Creation has nothing to do with science or scientific explanations; any competition here is based on misunderstanding and is misguided. Creation is a religious statement, a statement of faith that in order to understand ourselves and our world at our deepest level, we must be seen as a response to the life-giving word of God. We and our world exist most truly in relationship to God. "Creation" is a statement not only about temporal beginnings but about each and every moment of our lives.

Image of God

Within this world, we human beings, men and women, have a special role to play. On the one hand, we are part and parcel of the world, fully and deeply integrated into it; on the other, we are the climax of God's creative activity and are raised up to be image of God (1:26-28). Obviously, this is an extremely important concept for understanding our role before God and within the universe.

The first thing to note is that the Hebrews were forbidden to make images of God, "in the shape of anything in the sky above or the earth below or in the waters beneath the earth" (Ex 20:4; Dt 5:8). Why? We get a clue from the polemics against the idols which occur in various parts of the Old Testament (e.g., Jer 10:1-11; Isa 40:18-20; 44:9-20; Dan 5:23; Ps 135:15-18). Over and over we meet the same charges: the idols of the nations are ineffectual, they can do nothing. They have eyes but see not; ears, but hear not; mouths, but cannot speak. They are supposed to help us carry our burdens, but instead become for us just an additional burden that we must carry around (Isa 46:1-7). In a word, the idols are dead. The living God of Israel can be imaged only by living beings who do what God does. God wants us humans to be that image.

What is involved in this? How do we go about it? Two things are essential. First, we must recognize and accept being an image. To be an image is to reflect another who comes first, another with whom we are tightly bound in relationship. This means we are not number one, but number two. This involves on our part a humble recognition of creaturehood and of limitation; a recognition that we, and all the relations to others and to the material world which make up our lives, exist only as gift. We are called into existence by, and are completely dependent on the loving and life-giving word of God.

Second, we must live out our imagehood. In the text this is specified in two directions: (1) "Be fertile and multiply; fill the earth, and (2) subdue it. Have dominion over the fish of the sea, the birds of the air, and all the living things that move on the earth" (1:28). In other words, we image God by doing exactly what we have just seen God doing. To "be fertile and multiply," to procreate, is to share in and reflect God's life-giving, begetting activity that was seen in the second panel of creation. However, since God's begetting life is done not through procreation but through the speaking of the word, procreation, while an obvious way, cannot be the only way in which we image God's life-giving. It is manifested also in all our concerns for life and the quality of life.

In the first panel of creation, we saw God subduing the dark, watery chaos; bringing an ordered, habitable universe out of the formlessness and void. In this way, God exercises dominion. As humans, men and women, we image God by sharing in life-giving and dominion activity.

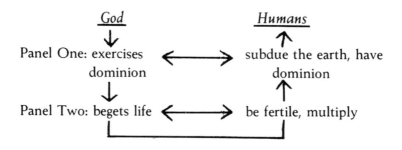

The aspect of sharing God's dominion can be elucidated further. It appears prominently, in words echoing our passage, in Psalm 8. Dominion, ruling, is a royal activity; in creating, God is exercising kingship. This theme, too, appears in the psalms (e.g., Ps 93, 96-99). In royal contexts two terms occur especially frequently to describe the task and obligation of the king to maintain an orderly realm in which peoples and nature can live in harmony and right relationship. These two terms are justice (*sedaqa*) and peace (*shalom*). Both of these point to integrity, wholeness and harmony and are the opposite of chaos (see, e.g., Isa 9:5-6; 11:1-9; Ps 72). To share dominion, then, implies and includes working to build and maintain a universe marked by right relations and peaceful order. If instead we produce a world torn by social strife and ecological crisis, it is clear we have failed miserably to live and have dominion in God's image.

To summarize: To be God's image involves two things: (1) that we accept the fact that we are image, and (2) that we reflect God's activity in our lives by being life-giving, justice-doing and peace-making (i.e., sharing dominion). Later theology and spirituality will speak of these two dimensions of our call in other terms. (1) To accept imagehood is an act of *faith*. By faith, we recognize our complete dependence on God, accept ourselves and our world as gifts of our God, and open ourselves to receive of God's fulness. (2) To live it out is an act of *charity*. By charity, we work to express and restore, where broken, the unity, the oneness of ourselves with each other, with all of creation and with God. If we really have faith in the God we say we do, it will be manifested in our lives; and conversely, the lives we live, the values we embody, will manifest who our God really is. The two are flip sides of the same coin and embody the call to be image of God.

The Failure of Imagehood

The basic spiritual question becomes, then, how do we image our God? The stories which immediately follow suggest that we do it rather poorly. Gen 2:4b-11:26 has traditionally been called the "primeval history," but we need to be alert to the fact that we are not dealing here with history in the modern sense of the term. These chapters deal, above all, with basic, paradigmatic aspects of our religious position before God.

Generally considered, four basic stories occur in these chapters: (1) Adam and Eve (2:4b-3:24); (2) Cain and Abel (4:1-26); (3) Noah and the Flood (6:1-9:29); and (4) the Tower of Babel (11:1-9). Interspersed among and connecting these stories are various geneologies (e.g., chapters 5; 10; 11: 10-26). If we look at these as a unit, we will discover that each really tells only one, same, basic story: (A) humans sin; (B) punishment follows, but (C) the last word is one of grace from God.

(A) HUMANS SIN

In each of the stories, the trouble begins with human sin. Adam and Eve eat of the fruit of the forbidden tree (2:16-17; 3:1-7); what kind of fruit is not mentioned and is immaterial. The man and the woman together violate God's command. Cain assumes to himself power over life and kills his brother, Abel (4:8). The generation of the flood fills the earth with wickedness and lawlessness (6:5, 11). The Hebrew word often translated "lawlessness" or "violence" (*hamas*) is very often used to describe various forms of social injustice (e.g., Mic 6:10-12). Finally, the people of Shinar (in Babylonia) want to make for themselves a great city, a great tower, and a great name (11:4).

While the modalites vary, the sin in each of these stories is one and the same; as human beings we overstep the limits of creaturehood and play God. In other words, we reject image-hood; we would rather be number one! The snake spells this out clearly for Adam and Eve, "You will become (like) gods!" (3:5). And what happens when we do this?

(B) PUNISHMENT

In each story, human violation of imagehood is followed by a punishment. For Adam and Eve, it is basically death (2:17; 3:19). Cain is made to wander alone over the earth (4:12). The flood comes destroying the sinful generation and with them all other living things (7:6-8:14). At the tower of Babel, the people are scattered, and their languages are confused (11:7-9).

We just saw that in all of the stories, the sin is one and the same. Here we note that the punishment is also really one and the same, and it, too, is named in the first story: "the moment you eat . . . you will die" (2:17). The punishment is death, but here we have a problem. For us, death usually refers to the moment of our last breath on earth; for the Bible, however, this is much too narrow. In the creation story we saw God call into being an ordered and harmonious universe, one in which life is possible; everything exists in right relationships. Death is the breaking and collapse of all these relationships on all their levels. Death is not just a moment at the end, but a whole realm of brokenness that affects our lives on many levels.

This realization can help us deal with a difficulty which arises immediately in the Adam and Eve story. They are told that at the very moment they eat of the tree, they will die (2:17). They eat and go on living for a long time, Adam for 930 years (5:5)! What is happening here? The fact is that the very moment they ate, they did die. The process began. They realized their nakedness and were ashamed (3:7); they hid from God (3:8); they argued and blamed each other (3:9-12). The harmonious relationship between man and woman was broken; it would end in subjection (3:16). This does not represent God's purpose, but the reality of death and brokenness in our lives. To seek to perpetuate such subjection in the name of religion is surely a travesty. Further, the relationship to animals, represented by the snake, is cursed (3:14), as is the relationship to the earth itself, which now gives life (produce) only with difficulty (3:17). With sin, all our other relationships break down. Curse is the power of death, as blessing is the power of life.

In the rest of the stories, death is manifested in diverse ways. The first death recorded, that of Abel, is not a "natural" death at a ripe old age, but a sinful death, a murder. Since Cain cannot live in peace with his brother, he must wander alone, separated, out of community (4:12). Human injustice (*hamas;* 6:11) breaks down and destroys the social order; the cosmic order likewise collapses. Life and the created order are broken and return to chaos. The rain is not "plain old rain," but the return of the primordial waters of chaos subdued by God in creation (7:11). With profound insight, the tower of Babel story recognizes that the scattering of people and their inability to communicate, to speak with each other is likewise a manifestation of death, of brokenness. Even the geneologies contribute to the picture. Broadly speaking, people in these listings start off living long, long lives, but then the life-spans get shorter and shorter. In other words, the power of death is getting stronger; it grabs humans sooner and sooner. We are made for communion, for "union-with," with ourselves, with others, with material creation and with God. In its place we have brokenness and "ex-communion." All this is covered by the biblical view of death.

One further dimension of this punishment of death needs to be noted. Even though God is depicted as intervening and speaking a sentence, the punishment is not arbitrary and imposed from the outside. The punishment flows from and expresses the inner nature of the sin. We humans are created from the life-giving word of God and breathe with the breath of God (2:7). To reject God is to turn our back on the source of our life; it is to reach out and turn off our air supply. What is the cutting off of life but death? Since we have broken our relationship with God, the source of life, our relationships with ourselves, other persons, the animal world, natural creation itself, all begin to come apart. In place of life, peace and justice, we return to chaos. Death is not an arbitrary punishment for sin, it is an expression, a "sacrament," of what sin really and truly is. Our last breath is simply the last step.

As human beings, we men and women are called (1) to accept being God's image, and (2) to live it out in our concern for life-giving, peace-making and justice-doing (dominion). These stories show graphically that when we (1) reject being image and play God, (2) we become instead death-giving, strife-making and injustice-doing. The two are indeed flip sides of the same coin.

(C) GOD'S GRACE

God brings order into the world and fills it with life; we bring death and brokenness and chaos. Who will have the last word? Whose will "will be done"? Each of the stories leaves us in no doubt: God's will for life and blessing prevail. Immediately after the sentence of death, Eve is named the "mother of all the living" (3:20), and God makes garments to cover their shame (3:21). Cain fears that he too will be killed, so God puts a mark on him (a tribal tatoo?) as a sign of care and protection (4:15). Noah, a righteous man, and his family and some animals survive the flood and are the source of new life on the earth; God promises not to destroy the earth again (8:21-22). The tower of Babel seems to lack a comparable sign of grace, but does it really? The call of Abraham which follows marks a further step in God's new beginning. God still wills life and blessing for creation.

Abraham: Model of Faith

"The Lord said to Abram: 'Go forth from the land of your kinsfolk and from your father's house to a land that I will show you. I will make of you a great nation, and I will bless you; I will make your name great so that you will be a blessing. I will bless those who bless you and curse those who curse you. All the communities of the earth will find blessing in you.' Abram went as the Lord directed him . . ." (12:1-4).

These words mark a turning point. The steady spread of curse, of the power of death, by human beings who betray their call to imagehood, is about to be reversed. The spread of blessing will be a gradual process; it will call for a long period of education, but it begins with the call of one person.

"Go forth! Right here and now, in the present; let go of your past, your land and your family (the two realities which, then as now, make life both possible and meaningful) and set out into a new future, a future that I will give you. I will be present to you, and you will have a new land and a new family, but these will flow from your relationship to me. The power of life, of blessing, will be manifested through you and your family."

Abraham went as the Lord directed; he responded with obedient faith. God's original purpose for humans (be life-giving, have dominion over the earth; Hebrew, (*eres*) is focussed now in a special way on this individual (you will beget a great family in the land [*eres*] I give you). But the horizon is indeed universal: "all the communities of the earth will find blessing in you."

Because he trusted himself into the darkness of God's future, Abraham has been considered *the* model of faith. But his faith was not a static, once-for-all response. It had to be reaffirmed and deepened at later times in his life. No sooner do he and his family arrive in the land, when famine drives them out into Egypt; then Sarah, his wife, is threatened by Pharaoh. Abraham does not trust the promise but takes things into his own hands (12:10-20). The child of the promise is delayed; repeatedly Abraham tries to do things his way: by adopting Eliezer (15:1-6); by having a son, Ishmael, through Hagar, Sarah's servant (16-17). Finally, when Isaac, the son of the promise arrives, Abraham faces his greatest crisis: sacrifice your son (22:1-19). The hope of God's future, the promise of life, would seem to end in death. In his struggle and anguish, Abraham affirms his faith, and God reaffirms the promise (22:17-18) in words which echo and repeat the words of 12:1-3, 15:5, 17:5-8.

In all of this, Abraham, the great model of faith, emerges as a curious mixture of faith and doubt, of certainty and confusion. Is this consistent? In the Bible, faith is not viewed in the sterile and rationalistic sense of "the assent of the mind to certain truths or propositions about God." It is not the mind that believes; it is rather the person. Faith, in the Bible, is a loving, trusting commitment of the whole self to God, a holding on securely to God in spite of everything. At times we are confused; we struggle and doubt. This is not opposed to faith; it is part of faith, the part that says that we care enough about our relationship to God to question and argue (15:2-3) and even at times to laugh (17:17).

Jacob: Conflict and Reconciliation

The long awaited son of the promise proves to be a fairly colorless character in the story. Isaac, appearing as either Abraham's son or Jacob's father is primarily a transition figure. In Jacob, however, we meet one of the liveliest of the biblical personages.

While still in the womb, Jacob is marked as a figure of strife and conflict (25:19-26). The first of his opponents is his brother Esau, who represents Edom, the country to the southeast of Palestine and one of Israel's traditional enemies. Jacob tricks Esau out of the birthright which belongs to him as the first born (25:27-34); then, with his mother's help, he deceives his aged father into giving him the special blessing (27:1-45). Not surprisingly, Esau is none too happy about this and seeks to kill his brother: Jacob has to flee for his life (27:41-45).

Jacob leaves the land of Canaan and comes to Haran, far to the northeast, the city from which Abraham had earlier set out (11:31-32). There he falls in love with Rachel and goes to work for Laban, his father-in-law to be (29:1-14). Unlike Esau, Laban is rather shrewd himself and a more worthy opponent for Jacob's wiles. The struggle and deceptions continue (29:15-30:43).

Jacob has one final struggle. On his return to Canaan, he spends the night wrestling with "some man" (32:25). Only at the end does he come to realize that he has been contending with God. As he had been named "Jacob" because of his pre-birth struggle with Esau, he is now renamed "Israel" because of his struggle with God (32:29).

Two aspects of the Jacob story can be noted The first is that God's presence and promise are pure gift; they are not earned or merited. They cannot be based on a right, for example, the right of the first born. As Isaac was not Abraham's first born (Ishmael was), so Jacob was second to Esau. Nor can they be claimed by merit. Jacob is hardly a paragon of virtue, but it is precisely as he is fleeing from Esau's anger, the direct consequences of his own actions, that Jacob receives, in his dream at Bethel (28:10-22), the unexpected assurance of God's presence and the renewal of blessing. In the land of Laban these make Jacob prosperous and are manifested in the birth of the twelve children (29:31-30:24); they urge Jacob to return to Canaan (31:1-3). All are God's gift and cannot be claimed on any basis.

However much God may be with Jacob, secondly, this does not solve all of his problems. Jacob had made a mess of his relations with his brother, and had given as good as he received with his father-in-law. It is up to Jacob to begin to put these relationships right. *He* must make efforts of reconciliation with each of them. Laban pursues Jacob after his flight and presents his complaint (31:22-32:3). Jacob acknowledges his dependence on God (31:42) and, at Laban's initiative, agrees to conclude a covenant (31:44). While the terms of their mutual oaths point to possible problems in the future, the purpose of a covenant is peace, and the two do share in a covenant meal that expresses this (31:54).

Esau is another matter (32:4-22, 33:1-20). Jacob sends messengers ahead to plead for favor. When these bring back an ambiguous response, he again acknowledges his dependence on God and his unworthiness (32:10-13) and sends more gifts ahead. When at last the brothers meet, they have a tearful reunion (33:3-4). As they part to continue their journey, Jacob begins to hedge again, and instead of joining Esau in Seir, he heads for Shechem. Reconciliation there may be, but it is far from perfect.

In summary, God's presence and blessing go with Jacob as

gracious gift to which he can lay no claim whatsoever. But his presence does not take away Jacob's own responsibility. He alienated Esau and Laban; it is his task to seek some kind of reconciliation with both. In this context, Jacob recognizes and confesses his own dependence on God. And, interestingly enough, it is only after he has sought a peaceful conclusion to his other struggles that Jacob has his final struggle, with God, and becomes "Israel" in the process.

Joseph: Faith and Reconciliation

Just as Isaac grew old and had trouble with his children, so Jacob undergoes a similar fate. Because of the favoritism he shows to Joseph, his second-youngest son, there is strife and jealousy among the brothers (37:1-20). As a result, they plan first to kill him but then revise this in favor of selling him into slavery. Sold to some travelling traders, Joseph goes down into Egypt (37:2-36) where his fortunes continue their descent. Placed in charge of a large household, Joseph resists the advances of his owner, Potiphar's, wife. Thanks to her lying testimony, he goes down into prison.

After two years in these depths, Joseph finally begins to rise. Pharaoh has had a disturbing dream, and Joseph's skills at interpretation are recalled. He comes up before Pharaoh. In view of the dream's message regarding a coming famine, Pharaoh appoints Joseph to be in charge of all of Egypt. Now enjoying full power, Joseph stands at the heights (41:1-57).

When the famine strikes, all people from round about come to Egypt where, thanks to Joseph's wise administration, food can be found in abundance. Among those coming down are Joseph's brothers. He recognizes them, tests them and tricks

them into bringing Benjamin, the youngest son and his own
full brother, to Egypt also. When at last he makes himself
known to them, his surprised and fearful brothers, he assures
them of his good will. Their father, Jacob, and all the rest of
their families join them: they settle and prosper in Egypt.

Throughout the story, Joseph consistently recognizes and
admits his dependence on God. "How could I commit so great
a wrong and thus stand condemned before God?" (39:9) he
says, spurning Potiphar's wife. When Pharaoh asks him to
interpret his dream, Joseph counters, "It is not I, but God who
will give Pharaoh the right answer" (41:16; see also 41:25, 28,
32). When he marries and has two children, both of their
names acknowledge God's gifts (41:51-52). When his brothers
fear him, he assures them, "I am a God-fearing man" (42:18).
They may have intended to harm him years before, but Joseph
now sees that through all of this it was really God working out
a hidden plan for life (45:5, 7-9). Finally, when Jacob dies, and
the brothers fear once again, Joseph reassures them, "Have no
fear. Can I take the place of God?" (50:19).

Because he recognizes and accepts his place before God,
Joseph is able to accomplish two things. First, he provides for
the life of the land. In fact, this is why God had sent him on
ahead to Egypt, "for the sake of saving lives" (45:5-8), "for the
survival of many people" (50:20). Secondly, he brought about
reconciliation within his family. He had full power and could
have taken revenge and imposed frightful punishments, but
"Have no fear. Can I take the place of God?" (50:19).

Joseph appears, in other words, as the opposite of Adam and
Eve. Created for imagehood and entrusted with the task of
spreading life and sharing God's dominion over chaos, they
failed. They preferred to be "like gods" (3:5) and so begot
death, strife and brokenness. Restoring unity would now have

the character of reconciliation. Joseph, however, has no delusions; he is under God and he knows it. Because of this, he is able, through his dominion over the land, to be the minister both of life and of reconciliation; he becomes a source of blessing. But there is a shadow: Joseph is human like us, and his administration does contain the seeds of later problems (47:13-27).

Conclusion

At the beginning of any spirituality lies some conception of God and the human and of their interrelationship. Genesis shows us a God who exercises effortless dominion over the chaos, who calls into being a whole, integrated, harmonious universe and fills it with living beings. As human beings, men and women, we are called by God to recognize and accept in faith who we are. We manifest this by our sharing in God's continuing dominion over the chaos and by being life-giving. The primeval history shows how we fail, first by rejecting imagehood and then by producing death and brokenness in our world. In other words, we return the world to chaos. However, God's will for life and blessing will be heard. The first and most basic step in this direction is that we recognize and admit our creaturehood. Thus the first cycle of stories that follow presents us with Abraham who, in response to God's call, leaves everything and follows wherever God may lead. Later, in the New Testament, Abraham's obedient faith will be basic to Paul's argument (e.g., Rom 4:13-16) and the model for the gospel call narratives (e.g., Mt 4:18-22). The second story cycle presents us with Jacob who also, at times, recognizes his dependence on God, but the focus is more on the need to see and appreciate how we sow strife in our lives and must take the responsibility to be agents of reconciliation and peace. Finally, in the third cycle, Joseph combines both of these requirements. He is a person of faith who can then share in furthering God's purposes, giving life and bringing wholeness and peace.

The book of Genesis is about God and about human beings, all of them, men and women of every time and every place. It is about how we are called to exercise power in our lives and in our world, the power of being God's royal images, and how and why we fail. The book of Genesis presents for our reflection and meditation the fortunes and misfortunes of imagehood.

❧

Suggested Readings

On Genesis in General:

L. Boadt, ROT, 109-154.

M. Maher, *Genesis*, (OTM 2, 1982).

F. McCurley, GELN, 9-63.

P. Viviano, *Genesis* (CBC 2, 1985).

R. Clifford & R.E. Murphy, "Genesis," NJBC #2.

On Creation:

M. Fishbane, *Text and Texture* (New York: Schocken, 1979) 3-16.

M. Guinan, "Creation, Evolution and Genesis: A Fair Fight?" *New Catholic World* 228 #1363 (Jan/Feb 1985) 26-29.

C. Hyers, *The Meaning of Creation: Genesis and Modern Science* (Atlanta: John Knox Press, 1984).

C. Westermann, *Creation* (Philadelphia: Fortress, 1974).

On the Failure of Imagehood:

> M. Fishbane, *Text and Texture*, 17-39.
> D. Clines, TP, 61-79 (also in CBQ 38 [1976] 483-507).

On Abraham and the Struggle of Faith:

> R. Davidson, *The Courage to Doubt: Exploring an Old Testament Theme* (London: SCM Press, 1983) 40-53.

On Jacob:

> M. Fishbane, *Text and Texture*, 40-62.

On Joseph:

> B. Dahlberg, "The Unity of Genesis," *Literary Interpretation of Biblical Narratives vol.* 2 (K. Gros Louis, ed.; Nashville: Abingdon, 1982) 126-33. An earlier form of this appeared as "On Recognizing the Unity of Genesis," TD 24 (1976) 360-67.

On the Overall Movement of Genesis:

> R.Cohn, "Narrative Structure and Canonical Perspective in Genesis," JSOT, 25 (1983) 3-16.

3

Exodus: Freedom From and Freedom For

The book of Exodus continues the saga of the Israelite people. At the end of Genesis, the Joseph story showed how Jacob and his descendants and their families left the land of Canaan and migrated to Egypt, settling down there and eventually prospering. God's promise of blessing, of a large family, begins to be fulfilled: they become a great and numerous people (Ex 1:7). They are, however, out of the land; this part of God's promise hangs suspended. What is more, it is precisely because of God's blessing, manifested in their growth, that the Egyptians fear the Israelites and begin to oppress them. The book of Exodus recounts the story of how God delivers them from this oppression, and how they set out on their journey to the land of Canaan. The word "exodus," in fact, means literally "out on the road."

They Groaned and Cried Out

The Egyptians reduced the Israelites to cruel slavery, making life very bitter for them (1:13-14). "Still the Israelites *groaned* and *cried out* because of their slavery, and their *cry for release* went up to God" (2:23). In other words, they lamented.

Prayer of lamentation is fairly common in the Bible; the words used in the passage just cited appear regularly in such contexts. In the book of Psalms, more than fifty (or one third) of all the psalms are in some sense laments. "My life is spent with grief, and my years with *groaning*" (Ps 31:11); "Because of my insistent *groaning*, I am reduced to skin and bone" (Ps 102:6); "With a loud voice, I *cry out* to God . . . I *cry out* to you, O God" (Ps 142:2, 6). There is a whole book called, after its contents, *Lamentations*. Of Jerusalem, destroyed by Babylon, it is said, "all her gateways are deserted, her priests *groan* (1:4); the city itself *"groans* and turns away," (1:8); and "all her people *groan* . . . " (1:11). What is more "Even when I *cry out* and *cry for release*, he stops my prayer," (3:8). Jeremiah, in his so-called "confessions" (Jer 11:18-12:6; 15:10-21; 17:14-18; 18:18-23; 20:7-18) pours out his personal lament and anguish before God, as does Job, throughout the book which bears his name (chapters 3-31). We are perhaps less familiar and comfortable with lament than the Bible is.

What exactly is lament? It should not be confused with prayer of petition. Lament is a spontaneous, religious response to the incursion of death in our lives. Death, as we noted in the previous chapter, is not simply a question of the moment when we breathe our last. It is rather the whole realm of brokenness that affects our lives on all their levels and in all their manifold relationships. When we experience the pain of such brokenness, we *groan and cry out*. Lament is a loud, religious "ouch!"

Characteristically, a cry of lament is addressed to God. The God of the Israelites was known as a God of creation and of life; if brokenness, chaos and death are overwhelming us, it seems as if we are abandoned by God. "My God, my God,

why have you forsaken me?" (Ps 22:2; see in the New
Testament, Mt 27:46; Mk 15:34). The relationship to God is
so basic and so important that the lamentor does not hesitate
to cry out in pain, in confusion, and, as with Abraham, in
doubt. We may need to recover a healthy sense of lamentation
in our prayer.

I Am With You . . .

"As their cry for release went up to God, he heard their
groaning and was mindful of his covenant with Abraham,
Isaac and Jacob. He saw the Israelites and knew . . . " (2:24).
The God of Israel is a God who cares about the poor and
oppressed and who hears their cry. Who is this God? This is
exactly the question Moses is afraid that he will be asked when
he goes to the Israelites, "Who is this God? What is his
name?" (3:13).

The name of Israel's covenant God is Yahweh. In Hebrew,
originally only the consonants were written, YHWH. While
the vowels are not completely certain, the form "Yahweh"
enjoys a high degree of probability. The later Jewish tradition,
out of respect for the divine name, ceased pronouncing it and
substituted the word "the Lord" instead. This custom is still
followed today in most translations into English: thus when
we read "the Lord," the Hebrew text most often reads
"YHWH."

Much later still, Jewish scribes added marks to indicate the
vowels to be pronounced. When they came to these four
consonants (YHWH is thus at times referred to as the Tetra-
grammation, i.e., four letters), they added the vowels for the
Hebrew word, "the Lord," which was to be said instead. Some
centuries later, Christian readers misunderstood this and
created a non-existent word, combining the consonants of

YHWH and the vowels of "the Lord" (in Hebrew), thus producing "Jehovah." The word may be time honored by usage, but it is nonetheless based on a mistake; the name Jehovah never existed as such.

Was Yahweh a name new to the Israelites at the time of the Exodus? It is most likely that it was. "I am Yahweh, your God, who led you out of the land of Egypt." This becomes almost a stock phrase (e.g., Ex 20:2; Lev 22:31-33; Dt 13:6), the two elements are tied so closely together. Both Ex 3:11-15 and 6:2-8 discuss the name as something new at that time, and Ex 6:3 makes it quite explicit, "My name, Yahweh, I did not make known to them (that is, to Abraham, Isaac, and Jacob)." There are, however, texts in Genesis which show these ancestors calling on Yahweh by name (e.g., 4:26; 12:8; 27:7, etc.). These are most likely to be understood as theological, rather than historical, statements expressing the belief that even though Israel came to know Yahweh only at the time of the Exodus, it was in fact this same Yahweh who was calling their ancestors long before.

What then does the name "Yahweh" mean? Here we face an initial problem. When we ask such a question, we are asking for specific information, namely, of a scientific or historical nature. This is actually a fairly recent understanding. People have always asked "why?" and "what means . . . ?" questions, and these were usually answered, not with scientific information, but with a type of folk story which tells what that name (or place, or incident) meant to that group of people. The answer then gives us less a scientific meaning and more an existential one. The explanations found in the Bible are almost always of this latter sort.

Perhaps an example will help, taken from these same early chapters of the book of Exodus. What does the name "Moses" (Hebrew, *Mosheh*) mean? Scientifically, it derives from an

Egyptian word meaning "begotten-of"; thus, Ra-mses (begotten of the god Ra) and Tut-moses (begotten of the god Tut). Moses is a shortened form (the name of the god has been cut off) of an Egyptian name. In fact, many of the members of Moses' family have names that derive from Egyptian.

But Ex 2:5-10 tells us a different story. Threatened with death, Moses is put afloat on the water in a basket (the Hebrew word is used elsewhere in the Bible only in reference to Noah's Ark in Genesis). Pharaoh's daughter rescues him and names him *Mosheh* because "I have drawn him out (*mashati*) from the water" (2:10). The story involves a loose pun based on the Hebrew word *mashah*, to draw out. But there is more to the story than this. God, working through Pharaoh's daughter, draws Moses out of the water and into life; God, acting through Moses, will draw the Israelites safely out of the water (of the sea) and into life (Ex 13-15). Moses thus foreshadows in his own life what will later happen to the Israelites. The explanation given his name is not scientifically correct; it is much more important—and truer—than that. It tells us what the name "Moses" really "meant" to the Israelites.

When we return to our question, "What does Yahweh mean?" we have to bear this in mind. We can attempt to give a scientific or historical answer. Here the best opinion is probably that "Yahweh" is a third person, causative form of the verb "to be" and means something like "God *causes to be* (the heavenly hosts)"; it may well have been known and used in the religion of Canaan before the time of the Israelites. But this is of little or no interest to the ancient Israelites. The question was too important for that.

Two passages in the book of Exodus give an answer to the question, Ex 3:11-15 and 6:2-8. The latter text, simply recounting what it was that Yahweh had done for the people, gives a virtual summary of the Pentateuch. The meaning of the name is to be sought, not in linguistics, but in Israel's historical experiences with its God. The account in chapter 3 is similar.

Moses is afraid that when he, following God's instructions, goes to the Israelites, they will challenge him. "Who is this God? What is his name?" How should be answer them? God replied, "I am who am (*Ehyeh asher Ehyeh*)." Then he added, "This is what you should tell the Israelites: I AM (*Ehyeh*) sent me to you . . . Yahweh, the god of your fathers . . . sent me to you. This is my name forever" (3:14-15).

This is clearly an attempt to explain "Yahweh" by "Ehyeh." Efforts to draw complicated linguistic connections between the two forms are misguided; like most biblical name explanations, this is based on a loose Hebrew pun. *Ehyeh* is a first person, imperfect, simple stem of the verb "to be," and can be translated "I am/am continually/will be who I am/am continually/will be." Nor is this "to be" meant in an abstract sense. God is not giving, nor would the Israelites have been interested in, a philosophy lesson. What is at issue here is dynamic, active, concerned presence: "I am . . . to you, with you (see 3:12). I am present, caring for you. I am your God, you are my people (see 6:7)." Later, when the people have broken the covenant, God will say through Hosea, "I am not/no longer Ehyeh to you" (1:9). For Israel, what did "Yahweh" mean? It meant the God who was/is present to and caring for Israel; the God they had known in their history; the God who heard their cry of distress.

. . . *To Deliver You*

Yahweh's presence to Israel has a purpose. "Go and assemble the elders of the Israelites, and tell them: The Lord, the God of your fathers, the God of Abraham, Isaac and Jacob, has appeared to me and said: "I am concerned about you and about the way you are being treated in Egypt; so I have decided to lead you up out of the misery of Egypt into the land of the Canaanites . . ." (3:16-17). Yahweh is with Israel to deliver them. The narrative of the deliverance focusses on two basic stories, that of the plagues in Egypt (7:14-11:10), and that of the event at the sea (12:37-15:22).

The story of the plagues occurs in Egypt, in Pharaoh's home park, as it were. Moses, with his brother, Aaron, repeatedly visits Pharaoh with the request, "The Lord, the God of the Hebrews sent me to you with the message: Let my people go to worship me in the desert" (7:16). Pharaoh refuses this, and he and the whole country are hit with a series of plagues, mostly affecting natural phenomena and animals (water of the Nile turned to blood, frogs, gnats, flies, pestilence, hail, locusts, and darkness) but some touching the people directly (boils, death of first-born). Although there are moments of wavering (e.g., 10:7-11), Pharaoh's heart was obstinate; in fact, we are told that it was Yahweh who hardened his heart (e.g., 9:12; 10:1). Finally, with the death of the first-born, the Hebrews are sent out of the land of Egypt.

In reading this account, our first impulse is often to feel that the upcoming struggle is hardly a fair one. What chance does Pharaoh really have? This is not very sporting of God! This impression misses a bit the point of the conflict. What is clear to us today was not so clear back then. In the Egyptian religion, Pharaoh was considered a god. He embodied the Egyptian religion and the whole set of values, social and political as well, which flowed from it. From the start, the conflict is between two gods, Pharaoh and Yahweh, and their respective religious value systems. Pharaoh embodied slavery, oppression and the *status quo*; Yahweh, freedom, liberation, and the possibility of a different future. The issue at stake was: who is really in charge here?

The land of Egypt is dominated by two great realities: the sun and the Nile river. It was the regular flooding of the Nile which, when it receded leaving behind a narrow band of fertile soil, literally made Egypt possible. Without this, it would have been just more barren desert. Regularly also, the sun rose and set. Each night it entered the west, the realm of dead and of darkness, and at daybreak, it defeated the darkness once again and rose victorious to bring heat, warmth and growth once more to the land. Pharaoh was identified with the sun god.

This brief background can help us appreciate a bit more what is going on in our texts. In the first plague (7:14-24), the life-giving water of the Nile becomes death-bringing blood. The whole ecology of Egypt is turned upside down. In the ninth plague, darkness covers the land. If Pharaoh is the sun god, Yahweh simply reaches out and turns off the light switch. The two great realities of Egypt are completely under Yahweh's control. So much for the power of Pharaoh! In fact, Pharaoh cannot even control his own heart; Yahweh hardens it for him. And some people even thought that this was a god! Pharaoh is not truly humanized until he rises in the middle of the night to bewail his dead son (12:29-30). Who is in charge here? Can there be any doubt? The issue of idolatry, of being confused about who is really in charge will be a constant temptation for Israel, just as it is for us today.

As clear as the issue should have been, there was still one act left to play. Once the Hebrews had been sent away, Pharaoh and his servants regretted their decision. "What have we done!" they exclaimed. "We have released Israel from being our slaves!" (14:5). Pharaoh and his army pursued Israel and came upon them encamped by the sea. They were facing certain death at the hands of the Egyptians. Instead of death, however, Yahweh gave them life. This event at the sea was the founding act of Israel as a people.

With an event as crucial and as significant as this, we should not be surprised that Israel told and retold the story, continually deepening their understanding of its meaning. The accounts we have (Ex 13-15) do not give us the bare historical facts of what happened; they celebrated the victory of Yahweh and its significance for Israel.

To feel the impact of the texts in somewhat the way ancient Israel might have, we need to recall some features of the religion of ancient Canaan.The Israelites had come out of this background, and it was not only natural but inevitable that when they tried to express just what new thing God had done for them, they would draw on some elements of their old religious language.

The religion of Canaan was concerned with fertility and the agricultural year. Fertility is simply another word for "life." The life of the family depended on the life (fertility) of the fields (producing crops) and of the flocks of animals. Crucial to all this was rain, which both provided water to drink and "fertilized" the fields, enabling the crops to grow. Not surprisingly, the main god for the Canaanites during the biblical period was Ba'al, who arrived on his chariot (the dark storm clouds), giving off his war cry (thunder), and hurling his spears (lightning). In response, the earth shook under the impact. Anyone who has been in a dramatic electrical storm, especially along a seacoast, can appreciate how awesome such an experience can be; it was even more so for the ancients who lacked any of our modern understanding of weather phenomena. It is no wonder that they worshiped the storm god who brought the life-giving rain.

As suggested by the description of Ba'al's appearance (technically called a "theophany"), there were enemies to be dealt with. The opponents of Ba'al were two: Yam and Mot. Yam, which means Sea, represented the destructive powers of the sea which would crash against the coast bringing havoc in its wake. The coast of Canaan lacked any good, natural harbors; sea always represented chaos and danger, an enemy. Yam/Sea, often represented as a writhing sea monster (with seven heads), was also known as Leviathan or Rahab. As the fall storms arrived over the eastern Mediterranean, stirring up the sea and crashing into the coast, the Canaanite saw behind this a struggle for power in the world of the gods, between Ba'al (life, fertility, order) and Yam (destruction and chaos). The sea monster is defeated, split in two; Ba'al reigns/rains and there is life again.

Enter the second enemy, Mot (Death). Mot controls the hot, dry, barren summer when everything withers and dries up. Mot/Death swallows everything, including Ba'al. The rains stop, and the earth becomes a wilderness. Is this the last word? No. With the coming of the rains in the fall, Ba'al rises to life and confronts again his old enemy, Yam. Thus the Canaanites (likewise the Jewish calender today) celebrated a New Year in the fall, September-October.

The Israelites in the Bible borrow language from this background. We see a hint of it in the Genesis creation account where God divides/splits the waters of primordial chaos (1:2, 6). We see more than a hint of it in a passage like Ps 74:12-15:

> Yet, O God, my king from of old
>   you doer of saving deeds on earth,
> You stirred up Sea by your might;
>   you smashed the heads of the dragons in the waters.

> The cords of the nether world enmeshed me,
>> the snares of death overtook me.
> He reached from on high and grasped me;
>> he drew me out of the deep waters.

Interestingly, when the psalmist says that God drew him out of the waters, the Hebrew word used, *mashah*, is the same word used to explain the meaning of the name Moses (*Mosheh*, Ex 2:10) as we discussed above. Ps 69 also prays "out of the depths":

> Save me, O God,
>> for the waters threaten my life;
> I am sunk in the abysmal swamp
>> where there is no foothold;
> I have reached the watery depths;
>> the flood overwhelms me. (vv. 2-3)
> Rescue me out of the mire; may I not sink!
>> may I be rescued from my foes,
>> and from the watery depths. (v. 15)

This could almost have been prayed by the Israelites as they fled Egypt at the sea. It can be prayed by us whenever we feel likewise overwhelmed. Similar imagery appears in Ps 42:8 and 88:8.

The power of this imagery continues even today in a secularized form. Melville's *Moby Dick*, Hemingway's *The Old Man and the Sea*, and Benchley's *Jaws* (both book and movie) witness to this. But the origin of the language is religious, and it was used to talk about the new thing Yahweh had done for Israel, the greatest of the saving acts, the one which formed the central affirmation of Israel's faith. The people were preserved safely in the midst of "Sea" and were "created" as uniquely Yahweh's own. "I have witnessed the affliction of my people in Egypt and have heard their cry ... (3:7) ... I am

Yahweh, your God, who led you out of the land of Egypt"
(20:2).

Signs and Wonders

"The Lord brought us out of Egypt with his strong hand
and wrought before our eyes signs and wonders . . . " (Dt
6:21-22). "He brought us out of Egypt with his strong hand
and outstretched arm, with terrifying power, with signs and
wonders" (Dt 26:8). As part of their sacred tradition, their
sacred story, Israel recalled these great deeds Yahweh had done
for them in bringing them out of Egypt (see also Ex 3:20,
10:1-2; Dt 29:2, 34:11; Jos 24:17; Jer 32:20; Ps 106:21-22;
135:9). At a later period of suffering, they would pray, "As in
the days when you came forth from the land of Egypt, show us
wonderful signs" (Mic 7:15).

Customarily, we view these deeds as great miracles, and
they challenge and delight the Special Effects Department of
biblical movies and television shows. But when we say, "These
were miracles," we have something rather specific in mind.
For us, a miracle is something that goes so beyond the
causality of natural laws that it must be attributed to divine
intervention. This understanding presupposes a unified view
of "nature," and a concept of "natural laws" which operate
through it and which we basically understand. Is it fair to
apply this to the Old Testament texts?

It is always legitimate for us to ask the Bible any question
we want to; it is not legitimate to demand an answer. The Bible
may have nothing to respond; it may conceive things very
differently; it may push us to re-examine and rephrase our
question. The question of miracle is a good case in point.

The Old Testament does not have a unified view of nature.

> You crushed the heads of Leviathan,
>> and made food of him for the dolphins.
> You split open (*baqa'*) the springs and torrents;
>> you brought dry land out of the primeval waters....

and in Ps 89:10-12:

> You rule over the surging of Sea
>> you still the swelling of its waves.
> You have crushed Rahab with a mortal blow;
>> with your strong arm you have scattered your enemies.
> Yours are the heavens, and yours is the earth;
>> the world and its fulness you have founded;

In these texts, the primary reference is to God's activity in creating the world. It is creation language.

We find the same imagery used to describe God's redeeming activity, delivering the Israelites from the Egyptians at the sea (Yam). It is very clear in a text like Isa 51:9-10:

> Awake, awake, put on strength,
>> O arm of the Lord!
> Awake as in the days of old,
>> in ages long ago!
> Was it not you who crushed Rahab,
>> you who pierced the dragon?
> Was it not you who dried up Sea
>> the waters of the great deep,
> Who made the depths of the sea into a way
>> for the redeemed to pass over?

or in one like Ps 77:14-21.

It also lies behind the description in Ex 14-15. The old poem in Ex 15 uses the language of the storm (wind, crashing waves, 15:7-8, 10) over Sea/Flood Waters/Mighty Waters (15:1, 4, 5, 8, 10). Likewise, God delivers the Israelites by splitting (*baqa'*; Ex 14:16, 21) Sea and producing dry land "for the redeemed to pass over" (Isa 51:10).

A subtle sarcasm emerges in the detail that the defeat of the Egyptians happened "just before dawn" (14:24). As noted above, in the Egyptian religion, the sun god, travelling during the night through the land of darkness, defeats darkness "just before dawn" and rises victorious to the new day. It is precisely at the moment when Pharaoh (the sun god) should be victorious that he is soundly defeated by Yahweh.

In all of this, the biblical accounts are telling us something very important about the meaning of the event at the sea. First, Yahweh alone is God. The Egyptian god (Pharaoh) is powerless; the Canaanite god, Sea, is no threat but is simply Yahweh's weapon against the Egyptians. Secondly, this Yahweh delivers this people, guiding them safely in the midst of chaos and destruction (i.e., with the sea on either side of them, 14:22, 29). Yahweh "creates" the people, giving them life in place of the certain death they were facing. Israel does nothing, but receives the gracious gift of life. We have left the world of mythology where gods struggle with each other for power. There is no struggle here at all, and no other gods to worry about. Yahweh delivers historical people, Israel, from historical enemies, Egyptians, but this deliverance is described borrowing the powerful symbols of the ancient religious world.

The same symbol of Sea as a force of chaos, death and destruction appears frequently in the prayers of lamentation in the book of Psalms. This is very appropriate because, as we have seen, lament is the response to being overwhelmed by the power of the realm of death. Thus we read in Ps 18:5-6, 17:

> The breakers (waves) of death surged round about me
> the destroying floods overwhelmed me;

One may speak of "everything," or of "the heavens and the earth = everything)," but biblical Hebrew does not even have a word for "nature." Neither does it have our concept of "natural law." The ancients were certainly aware of regularities and patterns in nature and human experience, but these were not quite as fixed as our "natural laws." The Bible, then, viewing things very differently, does not, and cannot, give us an easy "Yes or No" answer to our question.

The Bible does, however, call these great acts of Yahweh something: they are "signs and wonders." A "sign" is an event which points within itself to some deeper meaning; a "wonder" is something which draws our attention; we look at it with awe and amazement; it is special. These great acts of Yahweh were wonder-ful and sign-ificant, filled with meaning. Whether they were also miraculous in our modern sense is simply not answered or answerable from the texts.

The Bible's view of "miracle" is, in fact, rather the exact opposite of ours. For us, something which we cannot understand or explain is a miracle; it points to God. For the Bible, anything that points to God is a miracle, a sign, a wonder. The sense of the presence of God and the closeness of God in and through nature and experience was quite different from ours. God could, as it were, break out anywhere; anything (whether we today could explain it or not) could become a sign and a wonder.

We should not, however, think that because of this difference, the life of faith was easier for the ancient people of the Bible than it is for us today. The signs and wonders do not produce faith; much less do they "prove" faith (a contradiction in terms). They are perceived only in faith and through faith. If we had been at the sea with a video-camera, we would not have seen Yahweh in action; the Egyptians did not see and recognize Yahweh delivering the Israelites. This was an affirmation made by Israel, expressing its faith in its God. Their understanding in faith of what God had done for them would have to be deepened. This began to happen at Sinai.

Let Us Praise the Lord

Israel's immediate response to Yahweh's having redeemed them was to sing and dance. "The prophetess Miriam, Aaron's sister, took a tambourine in her hand, while all the women went out after her with tambourines, dancing, and she led them in the refrain:

> Sing to the Lord, for he is gloriously triumphant;
> horse and chariot he has cast into the sea (Ex 15:21-22).

The verses of the hymn are expanded considerably and attributed to Moses in vv. 1-18. Many scholars consider this hymn to be one of the oldest passages in the Bible. The Israelites responded with praise.

But what exactly is praise? It should not be confused with thanksgiving. Praise is intimately connected with life. One of the worst aspects of death is that it silences praise; there is no praise of God in Sheol, the netherworld, the land of the dead (e.g., Ps 6:6; 30:10; 88:11; Isa 38:18). Praise is the exact opposite of lament. If lament is the spontaneous response to the brokenness of life, a loud, religious "Ouch!," praise is a response to the blessings of life, a loud, religious "Wow!"

An example may be more helpful than a definition. When my youngest nephew was two and a half years old, I gave him for Christmas a purple teddy bear. When he opened it, his eyes lit up, and he ran around the room, crying, "Mama, papa, look! Uncle Mike gave me a purple teddy bear!" Only later, with parental urging, did he come over and say "thank you." If he had not, I doubt if I would have noticed; I had something better than thanks.

"Mama, papa, look! Uncle Mike gave me a purple teddy bear!" is praise. It is spontaneous; it calls to others; it focusses on the giver and the gift. The self is present only as the recipient, grammatically, the indirect object. (In thanksgiving, "I" thank "you." The self becomes the subject of the sentence.) These are all essential elements and are common features of the psalms of praise. They are present here in Ex 15. The people sing and dance, and call to each other to join in. Attention is on the giver, Yahweh, and the gift, deliverance from Egypt (vv. 1-10, 21). Israel has been blessed, gifted with life. In the words of the great Jewish writer, Abraham Heschel, "Prayer is our humble response to the inconceivable surprise of living."

Sinai: Theophany

Gifted with new and unexpected life, the Israelites journeyed from the sea into the desert where they faced a variety of problems. We will examine these later, in our next chapter on the wandering in the wilderness. Eventually they came to Sinai and stayed there for some time. This large section (Ex 19-Nm 10) forms the center and heart of the Pentateuch. It was at Sinai that Israel had an experience of God's presence (theophany), entered into covenant with their God, and received the covenant law. We will look at each of these in turn.

As the Hebrew slaves fled from Egypt, they had an experience of Yahweh's saving power at the sea. Now, at Sinai, they had another experience of God. The awesome appearance of God is described in the classic language of the appearance of the storm god, with dark clouds, thunder and lightning. "On the morning of the third day there were peals of thunder and lightning, and a heavy cloud over the mountain, and a very loud trumpet blast, so that all the people in the camp trembled . . . Mount Sinai was all wrapped in smoke, for the Lord came down upon it in fire. The smoke rose from it as though from a furnace, and the whole mountain trembled violently" (19:16, 18), Because of the traditional and stereotyped nature of this description, it is hard for us to say with certainty exactly what happened, but it seems clear that the people had a profound experience of the power and presence of God.

In the light of this experience, as well as that of the Exodus, and under Moses' leadership, the Israelites came to realize that Yahweh was their *go'el* (redeemer). What exactly was a *go'el*? Ancient families and tribes had a strong sense of solidarity, entailing the obligation to help and protect one another in times of need. In Israel, this obligation was connected with the office of *go'el*, redeemer or recoverer, who, as next of kin, had the duty to safeguard the life and integrity of the family or tribe. Thus, if property was alienated, the *go'el* should buy it back (Lev 25:25; Jer 32:6-7); if a family member is sold into slavery, the *go'el* should free him (Lev 25:47-49); if a man in the tribe dies childless, the *go'el* should beget children with the widow in the name of the deceased so that his name and property will stay within the family (this is the "levirate law"; see Dt 25:5-10; Gen 38:8; Ruth 2:20; 3:12; 4:4). Perhaps the closest comparison in our society would be the Mafia godfather, which comes out of a similar family social setting, with a similar sense of solidarity and obligation to protect the weaker members of the family.

If Yahweh was their *go'el* (e.g., Ex 6:6; 15:13) what did this mean? It meant that Israel and Yahweh formed one family. Yahweh was freely bound to Israel and accepted them as relatives and kin. As a faithful family member then, Yahweh had assumed the role of *go'el* and redeemed Israel from the slavery and bondage of Egypt. This profound recognition of kinship with Yahweh will find expression also in the ritual actions which seal the covenant (Ex 24).

Would it be proper to describe Israel's faith in Yahweh at this time as a monotheism? If we understand the word "monotheism" in a philosophical sense, i.e., only one God exists, then it is clear that Israel's early faith is not a monotheism; other gods do continue to exist. The first commandment is an indication of this: "I, the Lord, am your God . . . you shall not have other gods besides me" (Ex 20:2-3; see also Ex 18:11; Jdgs 11:24). It was because the other gods continued to exist that they continued to be a source of temptation to Israel throughout its history. Yahweh alone is God; while the other gods may continue to exist, they are out of work. Yahweh puts them in the unemployment line. The seeds of a full monotheism are here, but it will be some time before the existence of other gods is denied. Scholars term this, variously, incipient, practical, or implicit monotheism.

Sinai: Covenant

Israel recognized Yahweh as its *go'el* and they entered into covenant. We do not have anything in our modern societies exactly like the ancient covenant. The society of the ancient world was quite different from ours. Much of the social organization was one of clans and tribes; in some areas, such as

Canaan, smaller city-states existed. The relationships between these groups, e.g., between one tribe and another, between several city-states, between city-states and larger powers (e.g., Assyria, Babylon) which periodically arose, were obviously very important in regulating social behavior. Some measure of trust and confidence had to be established for the stability of social and political life. The covenant served this function.

A covenant was an agreement or promise between two parties solemnly professed before witnesses and made binding by an oath expressed verbally or by some symbolic action. Some covenants were written down and have been preserved for us, but this was by no means always the case. Covenants were closely connected with religion because the gods of the various parties were called on to be witnesses and also to punish any breach of the covenant which might occur. Law too was involved because either or both parties were obliging themselves to some particular and specific type of behavior. As a result of a covenant, a new relationship was established between the parties, a relationship often expressed in kinship terminology. Thus, partners to a covenant often were called "brothers." The goal of the covenant was *shalom*, peace, wholeness of relationship between the parties.

The Hebrew word usually translated "covenant" is *berith*. (The familiar Jewish organization, Benai Berith, means "children of the covenant.") It is not, however, a univocal term that always refers to exactly the same kind of agreement in exactly the same way. There is a variety of situations in which covenants appear and of forms in which they are expressed, some appearing in the Bible, some known from texts from the ancient world.

One type of covenant was the family-kinship covenant. In Gen 31, for example, Jacob flees from Laban, his father-in-law,

who goes quickly in pursuit of him. At Gilead they make a
berith (31:44-51). After setting up a mound of stones to
symbolize witnesses (a pun in Hebrew on the place named
Gilead), they swore an oath and shared a meal. Presumably
and hopefully, *shalom* was established between the two families.
Another possible example might be seen in Gen 21:22-33 and
26:26-32 where we see a dispute between Abimelech of Gerar
(a city in the Philistine plain) and one of the ancestors, in the
first instance Abraham, in the second, Isaac. A dispute over
water, that most precious commodity, breaks out between the
two groups. To establish *shalom*, a covenant is made. In the
first instance, it is sealed by an oath (21:31); in the second, by
an oath and a covenant meal (26:30).

Another important area of covenant activity, known from
outside the Bible, is that of international treaties. Larger
powers, such as the Hittites, the Egyptians, the Assyrians,
would enter into relations with each other or with smaller
city-states, their vassals; these relations were governed by
treaty covenants. Many treaties have been found, but especially
important are those of the Hittites (a kingdom based in central
Asia Minor) dating from *ca*, 1400-1200 B.C., and those of the
Assyrians, dating from *ca.* 750-620 B.C. (the so-called Neo-
Assyrian period). The structure and form of these treaties have
been analyzed, and many scholars are of the opinion that the
Sinai covenant, from the beginning, was modelled on this type
of covenant. Thus Israel, the vassal, was seen as having made a
treaty at Sinai with the great King of heaven. This opinion has
come in for some telling criticism, and here we prefer the
opinion that the earliest form of the Sinai covenant was that of
tribal or family kinship. It was only later, perhaps during the
Neo-Assyrian period, that the Sinai covenant was reinterpreted
in light of the international treaty models.

At Sinai, Israel recognized its kinship with Yahweh and there sealed a covenant which expressed that realization. The "concluding ceremonies" are described in Ex 24 where two ritual actions are significant: a blood ritual (24:6-8) and a meal (24:11, 5).

The blood ritual (vv. 6-8) might strike us at first as a little strange, if not actually bizarre, but we need to see it within the larger biblical context. A relationship existed between blood and life so deep that one's life was envisaged as inherent in the blood itself (Lev 17:11). To share the same blood was to share the same life; in other words, to belong to the same family. Moses sprinkled the blood on the altar, representing God, and then on the people; they have the same blood "in their veins." This passage, with its rich meaning forms the background for Jesus' words at the Last Supper (Mt 26:27-28; Mk 14:23-24; Lk 22:20) which are repeated in the Christian Eucharist: "This is the cup of my blood of the new and everlasting covenant."

The symbolism of sharing a meal to express and seal a covenant is likewise rich in meaning. Sharing a meal was a very important symbol in the ancient world and survives even today among many of the Middle Eastern Arab tribes. Eating the same food expressed belonging in some way to the same family and sharing in some way the same life. To harm someone with whom you have shared table-community was considered an especially serious offense (e.g., Ps 41:10). Community at table presupposes *shalom*, peace, harmony; enemies do not eat together. A meal ritual to seal a covenant appears, as we just noted above, in Gen 26:30 (Isaac and Abimelek) and 31:46, 54 (Jacob and Laban).

The reference to eating and drinking in Ex 24:11 suggests the covenant meal. A further reference may be found in v. 5

which tells us that holocausts (burnt offerings) were offered, and that bulls were sacrificed as *shelamim*, variously translated "peace-offerings" or "well-being offerings." These were sacrifices of thanksgiving to God whose characteristic feature was that the victim was shared. After part of the animal was burned for God, part went to the priest, and the rest belonged to the offerer who ate it at a joyful meal with his family and friends (Lev 3:1-17; 7:11-21). Here too the meal expresses a family sharing of life and *shalom* among themselves and God.

Sinai: Law

Before ratifying the covenant with the blood ritual, Moses related all the words and ordinances of the Lord, and all the people responded, "All the words which the Lord has spoken we will do" (24:3). Covenant involves obligation, so much so that one scholar has argued that the word *berith* really means obligation. We should not, however, view this obligation as something attached or added on from the outside. If flows rather from the very nature of a covenant. Because of the new relationship established, behavior changes. To put this into other words, Israel was gifted with life; the covenant expressed their family life with Yahweh. What do we do with life but live it? New behavior flows from the covenant life.

This new behavior was manifested in two areas of life. The first of these is the vertical relationship with God. Because the Hebrew slaves had been freed from the oppression of Egypt and adopted as Yahweh's family, their whole lives fell under Yahweh's control. They must live as Yahweh's people and special possession (19:4-6). Their deliverance from Egypt was not just a freedom *from*, but a freedom *for*. We are familiar with the old spiritual, "Go down Moses . . . tell ol' Pharoah, Let my people go!" That is in fact only half of what Moses told Pharaoh. The whole phrase (occurring nine times in the plague narratives) is, with minor variations, "Let my people go *so that they might serve me*" (4:23; 5:1, 3; 7:16, 26; 8:16; 9:1, 13; 10:3). The purpose and goal of the Exodus is Sinai.

Israel's first duty, then, was to be faithful to Yahweh. This is clearly spelled out in the first commandment, "I am the Lord your God who brought you out of the land of Egypt, out of the house of bondage. You shall have no other gods before me" (20:2-3). Israel owes Yahweh *'abodah*. The basic meaning of the word includes "servitude, hard work" (see below, Conclusion), but it comes to be the Hebrew word for "worship/liturgy." The God we worship is the ultimate source of our values and our behavior. The first step in forsaking the covenant is to worship false gods. Then, as now, the most basic sin against the covenant is not atheism but idolatry.

When Israel settled down in the land, they yielded to the temptations of the culture around them, and fell into false worship. The prophets spoke out strongly against this. Elijah would challenge the people who wavered between Yahweh and Ba'al, "How long will you straddle the issue? If the Lord is God, follow him; if Ba'al, follow him" (1 Kgs 18:21). Jeremiah criticized his people for burning incense to Ba'al and going after strange gods (Jer 7:6, 9); Ezekiel, for their eating on the mountains (at the pagan shrines there) and raising their eyes to idols (Ezek 18:5-6). Then they are brazen enough to come and worship Yahweh too (see Isa 1:12-16; Amos 5:21-27)! The Israelites had forgotten that they must serve only Yahweh and seek to "be holy for I, the Lord, your God, am holy" (Lev 19:2).

In striving "to be holy," the Hebrews realized that social

behavior was of prime importance also. The horizontal relationships with others is the second area affected by their new covenant life. By acting as *go'el* in their behalf, Yahweh had taken on and fulfilled a social obligation. The covenant at Sinai revealed an intrinsic connection between the nature of Yahweh and the demands of social justice. How Israel treated each other would be a sign and manifestation of how serious and wholehearted they were in their worship of Yahweh. A special area of concern here was the treatment of the poor, the oppressed and the alien. Like the widow and orphan, the alien, who lived in the land without any legal rights, was an especially easy victim for exploitation. The Hebrews had been poor and oppressed in Egypt, and Yahweh had delivered them. A motive frequently found in the laws for treating the poor kindly and not oppressing the weak is "because you were once strangers (aliens) in the land of Egypt" (e.g., Ex 22:21; 23:9; Lev 19:34; Dt 10:18; 14:28-29; 15:1-11). It would be the grossest contradiction for Israel, who had been redeemed from oppression by Yahweh, to become themselves oppressors of the weak and helpless.

And this was, of course, exactly what happened. Once settled in the land, Israel committed precisely these sins of injustice. Again, the prophets cry out in protest. Elijah confronts the king and queen, Ahab and Jezebel, over the theft of Naboth's vineyard, with its concomitant perjury and murder (1 Kgs 21). Hosea (4:2), Jeremiah (7:5-6, 9), and Ezekiel (18:6-8) all complain of lying, stealing, adultery and at times murder. Isaiah, Amos and Micah are particularly eloquent in their denunciations of the corruption of the legal system (perjury, bribery; e.g., Isa 5:23; Am 2:6-7; 5:12; Mic 2:1-3; 3:11) and the economic system (cheating, false weights; Isa 3:14; 5:8; Am 8:4-6). The Israelites had indeed forgotten that they were once poor and oppressed in the land of Egypt.

It used to be popular among scholars to see these two aspects of covenant living as separate and distinct. Thus we heard that the prophets rejected liturgy and worship in favor of an ethic of social justice. Today, one reads at times that the prophets called the people first to do justice, and only after that to worship. Both of these opinions are wrong and for the same reason: they regard worship and justice as separable. In fact, right worship is manifested in social behavior; social injustice flows from idolatry (regardless of what church we say we go to). In the prophets, their critique easily mixes the two areas together (e.g., Jer 7 and Ezek 18). The two areas, intrinsically connected, stand or fall together; they are flip sides of the same coin.

The two dimensions of covenant life can also be seen in a slightly different perspective. They represent further specifications of the call to imagehood articulated in Genesis 1:26-28. The first task is to accept imagehood, that is, to accept our creaturehood and dependence on the creator God. The Sinai covenant, adds that we recognize that all of our lives are the gift of the redeeming God who freed us from oppression and wants, in return, our sole and undivided worship. The second task is to live out our imagehood in and through all of our other relationships. Sinai focusses this sharply through historical memory: "Do not oppress others (work for justice) because, remember, you know what it is like to be oppressed! You were once slaves in Egypt." The Sinai covenant with its twofold obligation, is another step in God's educating us in imagehood.

The people responded, "All the words which the Lord has spoken, we will do" (24:3). Just before this, in Ex 20-23, we find the ten commandments and the so-called "Covenant

Code" (20:22-23:33). It is difficult to say how much, if any, of this material formed part of the original Sinai experience. Some of it may be quite ancient, e.g., the ten commandments (which form a concise summary of covenant life, the first several referring to our worship, the rest, to our social behavior). Much of the Covenant Code presupposes settled, agricultural conditions (e.g., 22:5-6), so it would seem to be much later. The book of Leviticus, which follows, with its regulations for sacrifices, priests, purification and atonement, and feasts, reflects a greatly developed ritual system. All of this is now included in the context of Sinai.

This whole "Torah" (Law), as we now have it, deriving from different periods of Israel's later history, was regarded as somehow being "given" by Moses. All of these later laws can easily be grouped under the heading of either right worship or of correct, just, social behavior, the two basic dimensions of covenant. If the covenant is to be, and continue to be, real and alive, it must relate to the real lives and problems of the people. Later generations of Israel, as they retold and relived the Exodus-Sinai story in their worship, naturally included new laws and regulations which made the covenant real for them by applying it to their new and different social situations. All of these developments are now attributed to Moses at Sinai because this is where the covenant began, and all the later developments ultimately derive their authority as concrete applications of the covenant which gave Israel its basic identity.

Rupture and Renewal

The people responded, "All these things we will do!" But it was not long before they didn't. Immediately following the sealing of the covenant, elaborate instructions are given for the construction of two items, the Ark and the Tent, both of them symbols of Yahweh's continuing presence in the midst of the people. But before they can be built, the people sin, and Yahweh's presence is brought into question.

The apostasy of the people is recounted in Ex 32, the famous story of the golden calf. The story is certainly connected with that in 1 Kgs 12:26-32 which tells how Jeroboam I, the first king of the northern kingdom of Israel after the split of the kingdoms, constructed two calves, one for the sanctuary at Bethel and one for that at Dan. However, in Exodus, the story shows us a typical Israel engaged in a typical sin; and that sin is idolatry.

Moses is delayed; the people are confused. They call on Aaron to make them a god to be their leader. He collects their jewelry and fashions a golden calf. After building an altar for sacrifices, he proclaims a feast. The people eat and drink and "rise up to revel" (32:6). Despite the excesses of Hollywood biblical epics, the reference here is more likely to some kind of ritual, cultic activity.

The scene cuts to Moses and Yahweh on the mountain, where an argument breaks out. Yahweh opens, "Go down at once to *your* people whom *you* brought out of the land of Egypt . . . let me alone . . . to consume them!" (32:7, 10), Suddenly, when they misbehave, they are *Moses'* people whom *Moses* brought out! Moses is not about to let that slip by. "Why, O Lord, should your wrath flare up against *your own* people whom *you* brought out . . . " (32:11).

Once that is clarified, Moses makes his case, scoring two basic points: "Why should the Egyptians say . . . " (32:12), and "Remember your servants," our ancestors, and your promises to them (32:13). In short, Moses argues, "What will the neighbors say?" and "But you promised!" Both of these arguments make more sense when we realize that the culture of ancient Israel was primarily an oral one. The society and knowledge within the society depended on spoken words; words counted and had to be reliable. Fidelity to one's own word was sacred, and what others said was the source of honor and shame. Moses carries the day.

When he goes down the mountain, Moses angrily confronts both the people and his brother. Aaron evades the issue in a fashion worthy of Adam and Eve in the garden of Gen 3. "This is an evil people! They gave me their gold which I threw in the fire. Then, out popped this calf!" Also, like the Adam and Eve story, the rejection of God for an idol leads not to life but to death. The people are punished, but the worst may lie ahead.

The next chapter, Ex 33, constitutes an extended debate over Yahweh's presence. "I myself will not go up in your company" (33:3, 5). By the end, after lamentation (33:4-6) and some hard bargaining (33:12-17), Yahweh relents. Moses sees God's glory and hears the name, "Yahweh (Lord)" as Yahweh passes by (33:18-23; 34:5). Yahweh will stay with Moses and the people, the covenant can be renewed.

The renewal of the covenant here follows the same pattern as before in Ex 19-24. The three elements of theophany, covenant, and law are present. Yahweh appeared to Moses, passed before him, and cried out in one of the most famous and important passages in Old Testament theology, "Yahweh, Yahweh, a merciful and gracious God, slow to anger and rich in kindness and fidelity, continuing his kindness for a thousand generations, and forgiving wickedness and crime and sin; yet not declaring the guilty guiltless, but punishing children and grandchildren to the third and fourth generation for their fathers' wickedness!" (34:5-9). Next a covenant is made

(34:10) and obligations are spelled out (34:11-26), which, as if to counteract the sin of chapter 32, are mostly of a cultic and ritual nature.

Then the Lord said to Moses, "Write down these words, for in accordance with them I have made a covenant with you and with Israel." So Moses stayed there with the Lord for forty days and forty nights, without eating any food or drinking any water, and he wrote on the tablets the words of the covenant, the ten commandments (34:27-28). The crisis has been passed; rupture has been replaced by renewal. The Ark and the Tent can be built. The book of Exodus ends with Yahweh's presence settled in the Tent, in the midst of the people (40:34-38).

Conclusion

The book of Exodus deals with two events in the history of Israel, the exodus from Egypt (Ex 1-15) and the covenant at Sinai (Ex 19-40). These events, which form the foundation of Israel's distinct identity as a people, can be viewed from a variety of angles. By way of summary and conclusion, we can look at them (1) as grace and response, and (2) as freedom *from* and freedom *for*.

A covenant was an agreement or promise between two parties, establishing right relations, *shalom*, between them. The two parties to the Sinai covenant were God and the Hebrew people. The initiative was with God who acted first, choosing the people and intervening in history to deliver and save them when they were enslaved and oppressed. Yahweh "heard the groaning and was mindful of his covenant with Abraham,

Isaac and Jacob. He saw the Israelites and knew ... " (Ex
2:24).

For its part, Israel responded to God's gracious acts, recog-
nizing that they were Yahweh's people, accepting the covenant,
and promising to live by its demands. The many laws, touching
on every area of life, helped specify how and what this meant.
As new generations faced new situations, new laws were
assimilated into the context of the Sinai covenant so that the
people's response might be wholehearted and up to date, that
is, in touch with the reality of their everyday lives. God's grace
and Israel's response is expressed concisely in the so-called
"covenant formula," "I will be your God, and you will be my
people" (e.g., Ex 6:7; Lev 26:12; Dt 4:20; 7:6; Jer 31:33; Ezek
37:27).

The exodus events recall how Yahweh delivered Israel *from*
the slavery of Egypt. The Egyptians had "reduced them to
cruel slavery, making life bitter for them with hard work in
mortar and brick and all kinds of field work—the whole cruel
fate of slaves" (Ex 1:13-14). The Hebrew root *'abad* means "to
serve with hard labor/slavery"; it occurs five times in the
passage just quoted. Yahweh is a God who hears the cry of the
oppressed and frees *from* such slavery.

But *for* what? The goal of liberation is Sinai. "Let my people
go so that they might serve me" (Ex 5:1, 3, etc., as we
discussed above, p. 63). The Hebrew root translated "serve" is
'abad; the Hebrews owe Yahweh their *'abodah*. We have seen
that this word comes to mean "worship/liturgy"; it is the same
word used three times in Ex 1:13-14 for "hard work/slavery."
Further, Israel is forbidden to enslave other Israelites because
"those whom I brought out of the land of Egypt are slaves of
mine, they shall not be sold as slaves to any one else" (Lev
25:42). This passage has clear linguistic connections with Ex
1:13-14.

As unattractive as it might be to say so, the biblical text is as clear as it can be. The goal of Yahweh's liberation is not simply "freedom" in any abstract sense. The Israelites are freed from slavery to Pharaoh in order to become slaves to Yahweh! The question is not "Slavery, Yes or No?" it is "Slavery to whom?" Slavery to Pharaoh (or any other idol) leads to death; slavery to Yahweh leads to life. Thus, true freedom is found only in slavery to God. St. Paul makes this same point exactly when he tells the Romans that they were once slaves to sin, but have become slaves to God (Rom 6:15-23). This is the same basic question as that of imagehood but now refracted through the experience of liberation from the slavery of Egypt. Our spiritual question remains: "Do we recognize who we truly are, and how we are to live?"

※

Suggested Readings

On Exodus in General:

> B. Anderson, *UOT*, 53-109.
> L. Boadt, *ROT*, 155-88.
> R. Burns, *Exodus, Leviticus, Numbers* (OTM 3, 1983).
> J. Craghan, *Exodus* (CBC 3, 1985).
> R. Clifford, "Exodus," *NJBC* #3.

On Crying Out in Lamentation:

W. Brueggemann, *The Message of the Psalms* (Minneapolis: Augsburg, 1984) 51-121.

M. Guinan, "The Ecstacy of Praise; the Depth of Lament," *Pastoral Music* 8:1 (Oct-Nov 1983) 17-19.

C. Westermann, *What Does the Old Testament Say About God?* (Atlanta: John Knox Press, 1979) 70-74.

On "Why?" Stories in Folk Culture:

R. Bongartz, "Masters of the Tall Tale," *Americana* 10:4 (Sept-Oct 1982) 69-72, esp. p. 70.

On the Plagues and the Deliverance at the Sea:

B. Batto, "Red Sea or Reed Sea?" *BAR* 10:4 (July-Aug 1984) 57-63.

F. McCurley, *GELN*, 73-84.

———————, *Ancient Myth and Biblical Faith: Scriptural Transformations* (Philadelphia: Fortress Press, 1983), 36-46. This contains an excellent discussion of the background of Canaanite language.

On the Biblical View of Miracle:

B. Anderson, *UOT*, 73-74, 81-83.

There are three articles (by J. Pierce, B. Malina, and J. Pilch) in *BT* 90 (Apr 1977) 1194-1212.

On Praise:

W. Brueggemann, *Message of the Psalms*, 123-67.

M. Guinan, "Ecstacy of Praise" *Pastoral Music* 8:1 (Oct-Nov 1983) 17-19.

P. Miller, *Interpreting the Psalms* (Philadelphia: Fortress Press, 1986) 64-78. (This appears also in *Int* 39 [1985] 5-19).

The Abraham Heschel quotation is from *Man's Quest for God: Studies in Prayer and Symbolism* (New York: Chas. Scribner's Sons, 1954) 5. This has been reprinted as *Quest for God: Studies in Prayer and Symbolism* (New York: Crossroad, 1982) 5.

On Sinai: Theophany:

E. Maly, "A *Go'el* In Israel," *BT* 98 (Nov 1978) 1757-63.
F. McCurley, *GELN*, 97-101.

On Sinai: Covenant:

B. Anderson, *UOT*, 91-95, 98-103.
L. Boadt, *ROT*, 173-184.
M. Guinan, *Covenant in the Old Testament* (Chicago: Franciscan Herald Press, 1975).
F. McCurley, *GELN*, 101-8.

On Sinai: Law:

B. Anderson, *UOT*, 95-98.
L. Boadt, *ROT*, 184-90.
W. Harrelson, *The Ten Commandments and Human Rights* (Philadelphia: Fortress Press, 1980).

On Rupture and Renewal:

B. Anderson, *UOT*, 103-6.
F. McCurley, *GELN*, 106-8.

4

Leviticus: Be Holy

At the end of the book of Exodus, Israel has survived its crisis of covenant, the Ark and the Tent have been constructed, and Yahweh is present in their midst. The picture there is calm and static. In Leviticus, the people bring their various sacrifices; the priests function at the altar and the Tent; the feasts are celebrated. The picture springs to life.

Leviticus derives its name ultimately from the Greek which suggests that it deals with matters pertaining to the Levites. Curiously, the Levites are barely mentioned in the book (25:32-34). In the Jewish tradition, it is known at times as the "Priests' Manual" (*torat hakohanim*), but even this is a bit misleading since few of the laws are addressed only to the priests (e.g., 8-10; 16:1-28; 21:1-22:16). Situated in the context of the Sinai covenant, Leviticus presents ritual and ethical prescriptions directed to all the people, as well as, at times to the priests.

The shortest book of the Pentateuch, Leviticus stands at its center and calls on Israel to respond to Yahweh, its God, in their worship and in their lives. Despite its obvious importance, however, Leviticus is a very difficult book for us to appreciate and relate to, divorced as we are by space, time, and culture, from its world of concerns. Here we will comment only on two areas, (1) the call to holiness, and (2) the celebration of the Sabbath.

Call to Holiness

In any religion, holiness is a very basic concept. Holiness belongs properly only to the divine; only God is holy. "Holy, holy, holy is the Lord of hosts!" (Isa 6:4). The threefold "holy" is one of the Hebrew ways of expressing the superlative degree. In addition to Leviticus, Isaiah and Psalms also stress the holiness of God (e.g., Ps 93:3, 5, 9).

This holy God has called Israel to be holy (Lev 20:26). "It is I who made you holy (sacred) and led you out of the land of Egypt, that I, the Lord, might be your God" (2:32b-33). In the Exodus, Yahweh chose Israel to be "a kingdom of priests, a holy nation" (Ex 19:6; Dt 7:6). Israel does not in any way win, or merit, or achieve holiness for itself. It is completely the gift of its God. Israel is then enjoined to be who it already is, "Be holy, for I, the Lord your God am holy" (19:2).

Within Israel, the priests are further set apart to be concerned about the holiness of all (8:1-10:20). The special task of the priest is "to distinguish between what is sacred and what is profane, between what is clean and what is unclean; you must teach the Israelites all the laws that the Lord has given them through Moses" (10:10-11).

We can thus see that holiness has a twofold aspect, one positive and one negative. Positively, holiness involves "attachment to" God, sanctification, living in a holy way. This involves both our worshipful recognition that Yahweh alone is the Holy One, and our manifesting this conviction in our relationships with others in our lives (e.g., ch. 19). Negatively, holiness involves a "separation from" what is unholy, unclean, impure, and sinful (e.g., 11:1-16:34).

For us Christians today, these laws concerning purity and impurity seem very strange and foreign; perhaps it is the case that we are prone to overspiritualize in religious matters. For Israel, holiness was rooted in the reality of creation itself. We saw above, in considering the creation account of Gen 1:1-2:4, that God does basically two things: (1) orders the chaos to bring about harmonious living spaces, and (2) fills these with living beings. This provides the rationale for many of the pure/impure distinctions. Thus, on the one hand, animals which seem to mix up or confuse living spaces (sea creatures which crawl in the water—11:10; winged insects which walk on all fours—11:20) are impure. On the other hand, the loss of any bodily fluids, especially blood, represents in some way a loss of life and so renders one unclean (chs. 12-15). While cases may exist where the exact reason is not clear, this concern for the proper ordering of creation and for the sanctity of life in all its manifestations seems to undergird much of the determination of cleanness and uncleanness.

The Tent of Meeting (later the Temple) with the Ark inside was the place of greatest holiness because it was there that God was especially present in and for the people. And in front of the Tent was the altar of sacrifice. Here, too, we confront an area where we moderns have difficulty. Our antiseptic world is far removed from the sights, sounds, and smells of this sacrificial slaughtering; the ancients lived much closer to the messy realities of birth, life, and death. The various sacrifices offered by Israel can be related to the twofold dimension of holiness just noted. They represent either a grateful recognition of God's graciousness, or a humble recognition of our sinfulness or uncleanness and our desire for wholeness once again.

The first words of Leviticus in Hebrew are *wayyiqra'*, "and (the Lord) called out." The call of the Lord to Israel that they be holy echoes throughout the book.

Keep Holy the Sabbath

In addition to its concern for holiness as expressed in sacrifices and purity regulations, Israel also had its calendar of feasts to help it recognize the holiness of time. The most important of the annual feasts are listed in Lev 23: Passover/Unleavened Bread (23:4-14); Feast of Weeks (Pentecost) (23:15-23); New Year (Rosh-Hashanah) (23:23-25); Day of Atonement (Yom Kippur) (23:26-32); Feast of Tabernacles (Booths) (23:33-43). Especially important though is the regular, weekly celebration of the Sabbath. Since this is so, a closer look at the Sabbath may be worthwhile.

We can begin by asking, "Why did Israel celebrate the Sabbath?" We find not one answer but two. The command to keep holy the Sabbath is the longest of the ten commandments (Ex 20:8-11; Dt 5:12-25), and the two accounts are very similar until the reason is given. In Deuteronomy (5:15), Israel keeps the Sabbath to remember how God had redeemed them from the slavery of Egypt. Thus Israel remembers that all their time is the gift of the redeeming God. When we turn to Exodus (20:11), we find a completely different reason. Israel rests to share in God's Sabbath rest of creation (Gen 2:3). The Sabbath is holy because God has blessed it, i.e., has filled it with life-giving power. Keeping of the Sabbath is a very sacred obligation (Ex 31:12-17) because in this way Israel remembers Yahweh, the Creator of the universe and the Redeemer of Israel. Keeping Sabbath is an act of memory.

Who celebrates the Sabbath? In the Bible, individuals are seen as living in relationships; my actions affect all my relations. Thus, "you and your son and your daughter, your male and female slaves, your animals, the alien who lives with you" (Ex 20:10; 23:12; Dt 5:14) all share the Sabbath rest. All those people whose lives are intertwined with mine—family, household, even aliens—are involved. The animal world also is affected. But it does not stop there. The land itself shares Sabbath, in the sabbatical (the seventh) year (Ex 23:10-11; Lev 25:2-7). Our Sabbath rest expresses an awareness of the interconnectedness of our lives, with other people, with the animals, with the natural world itself. We live from God's creating and redeeming activity and are called to extend and share this activity in and through all our relationships. Keeping Sabbath is an act of solidarity.

When do we celebrate Sabbath? Obviously, once a week, every seventh day. But every seventh year is a sabbatical year which involves the land in a special way (Ex 23:10-11; Lev 25:2-7), and every forty-ninth year (7x7) is the grand year of jubilee when the land lies at rest, property is returned to its original owner; slaves are set free (Lev 25:8-55). Sabbath is not meant to be an isolated occurrence, but it is to be woven into the recurring rhythms and patterns of the weeks and the years.

But what about times that are especially crucial or difficult? Do we rest then, too? Israel wanders starving in the desert. God gives them manna. Yet even here, in the midst of the wilderness, they are to stop and celebrate the Sabbath (Ex 16:21-30). Later, they settle in the land; there, the most important times were those of planting and harvesting. Food for the whole year depended on these. Yet here too, Israel is to stop and celebrate (Ex 34:21). We often think everything depends on us; we forget all too easily who is really the Source of all. Keeping Sabbath is an act of faith that our lives, our work, our time are, and continue to be, in the hands of the creating, saving, loving God.

Keeping Sabbath then is essential to keeping focus. We are pulled in many different directions in all the activities of our lives; it is easy to forget. Israel is to be holy, and the Sabbath is a great gift of God. It is blessed; it is filled with life; it is holy.

Conclusion

Leviticus teaches that "the life is in the blood" (17:11), and the book itself, standing in the center of the Pentateuch, can be seen as the heart pumping the life-blood of holiness through the people and all the relationships of their lives in space and time. We need to recognize and insist on this precisely because Leviticus is such a difficult book for us to relate to today.

This difficulty is true, in different ways, of both the Jewish and the Christian faith communities. With the destruction of the Temple in Jerusalem by the Romans in 70 A.D., many of the regulations for sacrifice and purification became impossible and irrelevant. While Jews today may pray for the restoration of the Temple and its sacrifices, attention is focussed more on keeping the Sabbath and the feasts, and on keeping *kosher* ("fit, proper") in cooking and eating.

For the Christian community, the religious institutions of Israel must be seen refracted through the person, teachings, life, death and resurrection of Jesus. Thus, for example, the older sacrifices are summed up and replaced by his sacrifice (Heb 9:11-10:18); the followers of Jesus are likewise a "royal priesthood, a holy nation" (1 Pet 2:9-10); Sabbath rest is sharing in the rest of the kingdom (Heb 4:9-11).

Whatever difficulties we face, however, the basic concern of Leviticus can still be heard, the call to "be holy, for I, the Lord your God, am holy" (19:2).

❦

Suggested Readings

On Leviticus in General:

L. Boadt, *ROT*, 188-90.
R. Burns, *Exodus, Leviticus, Numbers*, (OTM 3, 1983) 185-209.
F. McCurley, *GELN*, 117-22.
J. Milgrom, "Leviticus," *IDBS*, 541-45. This is especially helpful.
R. Faley, "Leviticus," *NJBC* #4.

On Purity Regulations:

B. Malina, *The New Testament World: Insights from Cultural Anthropology* (Atlanta: John Knox Press, 1981). Chapter 6, "Clean and Unclean: Understanding Rules of Purity," (pp. 122-152) is an excellent introduction.

On Leviticus and Christian Preaching:

L.R. Bailey, *Leviticus* (Knox Preaching Guides; Atlanta: John Knox Press, 1987).

5

Numbers: Wandering in the Wilderness

The Israelites' wandering in the wilderness actually began with their departure from Egypt (Ex 12:37; Nm 33:3-5). Rather quickly they came to the sea where the Egyptian host was destroyed, and the Israelites passed through to new life. After facing a variety of challenges and crises (Ex 15:22-18:27), they arrived at Sinai where they remained for the making of the covenant and the giving of the law. They stayed almost one year (10 months and 19 days). Having been carefully counted (hence the name of the book, Numbers) by Moses and his assistants, the tribes set out in an orderly march, actually more of a procession, through the wilderness. Progressing through stages, the march would end in the plains of Moab, just across the Jordan from Jericho, near the central hill country of Palestine, forty years later (Nm 33:48-49). The family of Jacob had departed the land to go to Egypt in a time of famine (Gen 46); they are now still outside the land, but poised, ready to re-enter.

The material in the book of Numbers is of differing kinds, from census lists and statistical information (e.g., 1:19-54) to priestly ritual regulations (e.g., 5:1-3; 15:1-41); from stories of the people's hunger (11:1-35) to arguments about Moses' leadership (e.g., 12:1-16; 14:1-10). The impression is not that of a continuous narrative strand, but of a series of separate stories, often with repetitions, gathered together to fill out the space of forty years covered by the wandering, and to present typical, recurring problems of the people before their God.

Forty Years

The people must wander in the wilderness for forty years as a punishment for their sin (Nm 13-14). They are encamped in the southern desert within easy reach of the land. Scouts are sent on ahead to survey the land, which they do for forty days (13:25), and to bring back a report of what they have seen. The land is described in glowing terms (flowing with milk and honey, 13:27), but a more serious note is sounded. Some of the inhabitants are large and imposing. The leaders, Caleb and Joshua, try to quiet the fears of the people and urge them to go up now, but they are afraid. They refuse and rebel against Moses and the leaders, and also against Yahweh. Their refusal to enter the land is a serious failure to trust in Yahweh's promise to give them the land.

Yahweh is angry and threatens to wipe the people out. Moses again has to intercede, using arguments reminiscent of Ex 32. A new element here is Moses' quotation of Yahweh's own self-description from Ex 34:6-7: "The Lord is slow to anger and rich in kindness ... " (Nm 14:18). Yahweh responds to Moses' prayers; there is forgiveness but also punishment, and one that fits the crime. The present generation had refused to enter the land; Yahweh refuses to allow them into the land. Instead, they must wander forty years, one year for each day of the scouting (14:34).

The number forty is a very familiar one in the Bible. In the story of Noah and the Flood, it rains forty days and forty nights (Gen 7:4, 12, 17; 8:6). After the sealing of the covenant, Moses is with God on the mountain for forty days and nights (Ex 24:18). It is during this time of absence that the people get restless and make the golden calf (Ex 32). After the covenant is renewed, Moses once again spends forty days and nights with God on the mountain (Ex 34:28). When Elijah is being pursued by Jezebel, he flees for his life and travels forty days and nights until he comes to the mountain of God at Horeb (Sinai) (1 Kgs 19:8). The number appears also in the New Testament. Jesus is tempted in the desert for forty days and nights (Mt 4:1-11; Mk 1:12-13; Lk 4:1-13); his ascension to heaven occurs forty days after the resurrection (Acts 1:3).

Numbers in the Bible are often not meant to be taken literally, but serve a symbolic function. Our suspicions are especially aroused with numbers that recur so frequently. What would be the symbolic meaning of the number forty? On one level, it represents a longer period of time. Here (Nm 13-14), all the present generation over twenty years old must die off (14:29). But there is more. The longer time has a content: it is a time of need, of struggle, of testing. In fact, there is also an extra-biblical occurrence in just this sense. The Mesha (Moabite) inscription mentions how Moab (the kingdom just west of the Jordan River) was oppressed "for forty years."

In the Bible, however, a third level of meaning appears. "Forty" denotes a period of preparation for some special action of the Lord; it is a time of grace. After the flood in Genesis, a new creation begins; after Moses' converse with God comes the renewal of the covenant. After Elijah's journey, God comes to him and enables him to return, strengthened, to his prophetic ministry. In the New Testament, after the temptations, Jesus begins the public ministry; after the ascension, we enter the age of the church. After the Israelites wander in the wilderness, they will cross over at last to the promised land.

The Wilderness

Since the time of the wandering is by and large symbolic time, what about the place? Israel certainly knew the real wilderness, since that would describe fairly well the regions to the south (Negev desert), the southwest (Sinai desert), and the east across the Jordan. The desert is a place of no water and no food since little vegetation can grow there. It is also the abode of dangerous animals; the jackal and the ostrich are particularly beasts of the wilderness, both of them noted also for their offensive noise (which makes Job's complaint all the more touching, Job 30:29; see also Isa 34:13; Mic 1:8; Lam 4:3, etc.). The desert is a place of extremes where the choices are more clear-cut.

But the wilderness also carries symbolic meaning, a meaning rooted ultimately in the religion of Canaan. As we saw above, that religion centered on the concern for life, central to which was the need for fresh water. Ba'al, the giver of the rain, was the most important god in their pantheon. Ba'al's second enemy, in addition to Yam (Sea), was Mot (Death). Mot is the god of the hot, dry, barren wilderness, and of the hot, dry barren season, the summer. He swallows down Ba'al; the rain ceases; the earth seems to be becoming all wilderness. The wilderness is a negative place where the power of Mot/Death holds sway. Of itself, it has no positive value. Even in the Old Testament, this would seem to be the case. Previously, scholars thought that some few texts reflected a "desert ideal," but more recent study has brought this into question.

Sea/River (another name for Yam in the Canaanite religion) and Death/Wilderness were the two big figures representing the forces opposed to the god of life and fertility. In taking over both of these images, the Israelites were asserting that only their God was the source of life and blessing. Yahweh brought them safely through Sea, guided and nourished them in the Desert, the realm of Death, and, when they finally enter the land (Josh 3:14-17), their crossing of River (the Jordan) is described in terms very reminiscent of the crossing of Sea (Ex 13-15). Neither Sea/River nor Death/Desert was any real threat; they need have no fear. Yahweh guided and preserved the people safely through both. The same two images will be used to describe the totality of Jesus' victory: there will be no more sea or death (Rev 21:1-4). The process in the Old Testament might be diagrammed like this:

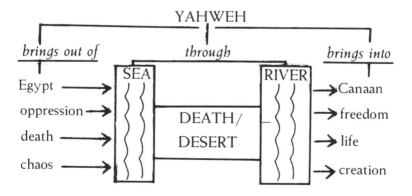

A *Time of Journey*

The wandering in the wilderness is not a time of aimless,

pointless movement. It is a journey, with a beginning in Egypt (Ex 12:37; Nm 33:3-5) and an end in the plains of Moab (Nm 22:1; 33:48-49). It progresses in orderly stages ("they set out from . . . and came to . . .") from Egypt to Sinai (Ex 23:37a; 13:20; 14:1-2; 15:22a; 16:1; 17:1a; 19:1-2) and then moves on from Sinai to Moab (Nm 10:12; 20:1, 22; 21:10-11; 22:1). A summary of the itinerary in Nm 33 mentions forty sites, probably to correspond to the forty years. Some form of the Hebrew verb for "to set out" (*nasa'*) occurs ninety-four times in the book of Numbers. There can be no doubt; the Israelites are on a journey.

Two temptations against the journey recur and have to be dealt with. The first is the temptation simply to stop, to settle down, to say, "That's enough! Let us stay here." In the course of the journey, the group did indeed rest. They do not seem to have travelled on the Sabbath; in addition, there were periodic resting places the longest (almost one year) being at Sinai. Another important resting spot is the oasis of Kadesh (or Kadesh-Barnea, Nm 13:26; 20:1, 16; Dt 1:46). But the time comes to get moving again, and they do this "at the bidding of the Lord" (Nm 9:17-18; 10:11-13). This is, in fact, a marked characteristic of the whole Pentateuch story. At the beginning, Abraham is comfortably settled in his land and with his family. God says, "Get moving!" (Gen 12:1-4). Near the end, in Deuteronomy, Moses recalls the departure from Sinai: God says, "You have stayed long enough at this mountain. Leave here . . . " (Dt 1:6-7). At the "bidding of the Lord," the community is forbidden to settle down too long. A similar theme can be noted in the New Testament accounts of Jesus' Transfiguration (Mt 17:1-8; Mk 9:1-7; Lk 9:28-36). The God of the Bible is a God who calls us continually out of secure and comfortable presents into unknown and risky futures. The journey continues.

In some ways, the second temptation is even worse. "And they complained to Moses, Were there no burial places in Egypt that you had to bring us here to die in this desert? Why did you do this to us? Why did you bring us out of Egypt? Did we not tell you this in Egypt, when we said, 'Leave us alone. Let us serve the Egyptians'? Far better for us to be the slaves of the Egyptians than to die in the desert" (Ex 14:11-12). This is a typical response of the Israelites in times of danger (e.g., Ex 16:3; 17:3; Nm 14:2-3; 20:4-5), or even in times of inconvenience ("We are tired of manna all the time! We wish we had a tastier diet, as we did in Egypt!" (Nm 11:4-5). "Why did you bring us out here to die? We would rather be back in Egypt!"

They do not want to stop the journey; they want to reverse it. They want to go back. Even though they have seen all the signs and wonders that God had worked on their behalf, they wish these had never happened! In other words, they wish they had never met and experienced Yahweh. They preferred the gods of Egypt.

This second temptation is idolatrous, seductive (especially for religious people), and very common. It is: nostalgia for the past. The past looks more attractive, more secure, safer. As well it ought! We have already been there; it holds no surprises; we know what it is. What makes the past so attractive is precisely the fact that it is past, and preferably, not too recent. "Why did you bring us out of Egypt? Did we not tell you this in Egypt, when we said, 'Leave us alone. Let us serve the Egyptians . . . '" (Ex 14:11-12). That is not exactly what they had said when they were there (Ex 2:23). Nostalgia depends on distance and selective amnesia.

We are indeed supposed to remember the past. We will examine this further in the next chapter. But when we do this, in effect, we are bringing the past into the present in order to help us live into the future. In nostalgia, on the other hand, we want to bring the present into the past in order to avoid the future. And how often this is justified by an appeal to the Bible! "Back to the Bible," we hear, "back to the Bible!" Do we ever hear, "Forward to the Bible?" When we go back to the Bible, what we find there is a God who is always out ahead of us, calling us into the unknown, into the future.

In our discussion above both of the meaning of imagehood (p. 26) and of the obligations flowing from Sinai covenant (p. 65), we noted a twofold dimension, one of accepting who we are before God (image and/or slave of God), and one of living that out in the context of all our relationships. We further noted that these may be related to the theological virtues of faith and charity (p. 26). Here we can now add the other of these virtues, hope. Hope directs us to the future; whatever the future brings, we can face it, confident in the life-giving presence of God. A failure to continue our journey into the future is, at root, a failure of hope.

We have looked at several general aspects of the wilderness wandering: the symbolism of forty, the meaning of the wilderness, and the significance of the journey. It is time now to look more closely at exactly what happened in the wilderness. We will see that it is a place of covenant, of testing, and of presence.

Wilderness: Place of Covenant

We might well ask, Why did the Israelites wander at all? Could not God have led them more directly into the promised land of Canaan? If God could defeat the Egyptians at the sea, why not along the "way to the Philistines land" (Ex 13:17) that lay closer along the northern shore? As we have already seen, the immediate goal of the Exodus was not to enter the promised land, though this may have been the ultimate goal in the larger picture. The immediate goal was "to serve me." The people went south to Sinai and to covenant.

But perhaps we can go a bit deeper. If a situation of oppression exists, there is a twofold problem: some people are oppressed because others are oppressors. As history eloquently attests, what usually happens when one group is freed from oppression is that the situation is soon reversed. The victims of today become the oppressors of tomorrow. This year's revolutionary becomes next year's dictator. Who will liberate us from the liberators? The root problem is that both th. slave and taskmaster most often share a common set of values. They agree on the most basic issues, but disagree on the present arrangement of things. When the slaves get the power, they become oppressors in turn, so the chain of oppression continues pretty much as it was. Is there any hope to break this chain which leads, not to an end of oppression, but to a game of musical chairs in which the "oppressor chairs" are just filled with new people?

If the Israelites, newly freed from oppression in Egypt, were to go straight to Canaan and assume power there, why would they be any different? Instead of Canaan, they went to Sinai for an extended period of "attitude adjustment." Covenant with Yahweh, the God who frees from oppression, called them to a whole different view of reality, a new set of values, and a totally different style of life. To live the covenant truly is to worship only this God and to be concerned for the human rights and social needs of others. These concerns are not intended as a luxury for the few or the prerogative of one political party; they are of the essence of covenant life with

God. Imagehood is about giving life, doing justice and making peace. The only way to break the chain is to become a slave of Yahweh.

When the Israelites finally did enter the land, they soon and repeatedly failed. But the covenant provided the framework and categories for understanding and evaluating their life and history; it also provided the basis for constant critique. The prophets, speaking squarely out of the covenant traditions, were able to appeal to something that all, the leaders and the people, could remember and understand.

Wilderness: Place of Testing

The wilderness was also the place in which Israel was tested in its fidelity to Yahweh, and repeatedly failed. This is often described as the "murmuring" or "rebellion" in the wilderness, and it started right away. No sooner had Israel departed Egypt and come to the sea, when they were afraid and longed to return to the "comforts" of Egypt (Ex 14:11-12). They had already seen and experienced Yahweh's concern for them and power over Egypt in the plagues. But obviously, this was not enough; so Yahweh delivered them at the sea. As soon as they set out, however, the complaining resumed (Ex 15:22-17:15). As a study in contrast, we meet the pagan priest, Jethro, Moses' father-in-law. Unlike the Israelites, who had experienced God's deeds personally, Jethro is shown to believe in and respond to Yahweh based solely on reports he had heard (Ex 18:1-27). At Sinai, under Moses' guidance, the people reflected on the deeper significance of what had happened, and affirmed and accepted this in their lives. But as soon as Moses was gone "too long," they fell away and made the golden calf. After the crisis of presence, the covenant was renewed, but once again, no sooner had they set out from Sinai, than the murmuring began anew (Nm 11-14). Finally, this generation went too far. Punished by God, it will not enter the land; that will happen only after the forty years of wandering are completed.

What is it that the Israelites murmured about? They are in the desert and have nothing to drink; God provides them with wonderful water from the rock (Ex 15:22-25; 17:2-7; Nm 20:1-13). They have no food; in their hunger they pine for the "fleshpots" of Egypt. The context, as well as the meaning of the Hebrew word, makes the meaning of this quite clear. In Egypt they had pots of meat to eat. The association of "fleshpots" with sexual sins has no basis in the text; it is an example of how the meaning of the English word, "flesh," has changed since the King James translation. God sends manna to feed them. Later, they grow tired of the monotony of the manna, so God sends quail (Nm 11:1-35).

The Israelites also faced dangers of another kind. First came threats from enemies without. The Egyptians attack at the sea (Ex 13:15); then the Amalekites (17:8-15; see Nm 13:29; 14:45; Dt 25:17-19). Later they will face Arad (Nm 21:1-3), Sihon and Og (Nm 21:21-35), the Midianites (Nm 25:16-18; 31:1-54), and others (Nm 32:39-42). After the departure from Sinai, internal struggles for power begin to emerge, struggles which had the potential to tear the young community apart. The disputes centered especially on the leadership of Moses and Aaron. The people wanted another leader, one who would take them back to Egypt; Moses and Aaron were the prime forces reminding them of their covenant and challenging them to fidelity (e.g., Nm 12:1-16; 14:1-4; 16:1-35).

The wilderness is a place of extremes, and choices are more clear cut. Food and water are essential for physical survival;

security from external threat and internal stability are essential for social survival. These are legitimate needs and concern for them is understandable, but in the biblical story, another element is added.

The presence of these various needs and dangers was the occasion for testing Israel's faith. Israel, both before and after Sinai, was a motley crew (Ex 12:38; Nm 11:4), united only by having shared two experiences: Yahweh's saving deeds in Egypt and at the sea, and the covenant at Sinai. A gradual build-up is noticeable in Israel's experiences:

signs and wonders in Egypt ⟶ murmur before Egypt at the Sea

deliverance at the sea ⟶ murmur for water and food

God gives water and manna ⟶ danger from Amalekites

God gives victory   — — — — —

↓

Arrival at Sinai

Israel has had plenty of opportunity to see that Yahweh both could and did take care of them; all the saving actions can be reduced to one: God is present with the people, and this is their source of life and survival. When they set out from Sinai and experienced the same kinds of needs again (some of the stories in Numbers seem to be doublets of those in Exodus), they really should have known better. Their murmuring then, coming after so much of God's care, became especially tiresome and annoying.

Crying out to God in times of need and distress is lamentation, a common feature, as we have seen of biblical prayer.

Some of Israel's cries to God are of this sort (e.g., Ex 15:22-25), but not many. "Why did you bring us out of Egypt? We wish we were back there" is not lamentation; it is a wish that the Exodus (and later Sinai) had never happened. Lamentation is an expression of faith; murmuring is a failure of faith, a fact which did not escape Yahweh's notice.

At Sinai, the people had affirmed, "All that Yahweh has said, we will do" (Ex 24:3), and they were, presumably, sincere in this. But were they actually able to follow through? Could they "unlearn" that quickly and easily all the values of their previous life? Before going into the land, they had, then, an extensive period of probation. In this period, the murmurings after Sinai are much more serious than those before. "This generation shall not enter into the land" (Nm 14:29-30); they did not pass their test very well. As strongly as we may say that we want—and really intend—to follow God, many forces remain, within and without, to pull us away from God and push us toward idols. It is always the most legitimate needs, e.g., food, water, defense, internal order, which can become the biggest idols. When they do, they beget, like all idols, only death. The wilderness was a place of testing.

Wilderness: Place of Presence

The wilderness was a place of threats to life and of death. Israel is tested to see if, in fact, they will truly believe that Yahweh, a God of life, is present with them there. Was their faith that strong?

In addition to their memory of God's saving deeds in their behalf, Israel had several other, more tangible and concrete symbols of Yahweh's presence in their midst. When Moses was "too long" on the mountain in converse with God, he had received detailed instructions for the building of two objects, the Ark and the Tent (Ex 25-27). After Israel's sin and the ensuing crisis of presence was resolved (Ex 32-34), the two objects were constructed according to the detailed plan (Ex 35:4-40:38).

The Ark was an ornate, portable, wooden box (the meaning of the Hebrew word). Its original symbolism seems to have been that of a portable throne for Yahweh. Israel was forbidden to make images of God (Ex 20:4-5), so Yahweh was conceived as invisibly present on the Ark. For example, when the people went out to war, Yahweh, on the Ark, went before them (Nm 10:35-36). Along this same line, it has been suggested that the Ark may have been used in worship services as a "portable Mt. Sinai." Just as Yahweh had been present there, with smoke and thunder (Ex 19:16-19), so Yahweh was present on the Ark, surrounded by smoke (incense) and thunder (the blowing of the ram's horn trumpet; Ex 19:16, 19).

Another understanding of the Ark developed later. It was the place where the tablets of the covenant law were preserved (Dt 10:1-9). This is reflected also in the prescriptions of Exodus (25:16; 40:3). Because of this, it is called, at times, the Ark of the Covenant, or the Ark of the Testimony (to the covenant).

The other symbol of Yahweh's presence was the Tent, also called the Tabernacle. It, too, was a portable shrine, set up outside the camp. There Moses would go to encounter Yahweh, to seek an oracle, to discuss problems, to speak "face to face" with God (Ex 33:11). For this reason, it is called at times, the Tent of Meeting.

Each of these objects reflected a theology of presence; the Ark, more God's presence to lead and fight for the people; the

Tent, the place where Yahweh was present for purposes of revelation. Some scholars believe that originally the two objects were separate, perhaps deriving from different groups within Israel. Be that as it may, our present text sees them as combined (Ex 25). At the beginning of Numbers, after the census of the people, the tribes are to encamp, deployed around the Tent. When they are on the march, they are to continue to be each in its own proper place (Nm 2:17). Thus the march through the wilderness took on the character of a solemn, liturgical procession. Both Ark and Tent are visible reminders of the continuing presence of God in the midst of the people. Whether encamped or on the march, they should not be afraid, because Yahweh was with them.

Closely related to the Tent of Meeting is the image of "the glory of the Lord" (e.g., Ex 16:10; 33:18; 40:34). This term is used also to describe God's presence. The imagery seems to have its roots, again, in the old Canaanite description of the appearance of the storm god, wrapped in dark clouds and hurling lightning bolts. In a similar way, the fiery glory of God is covered by a dark cloud. When the cloud is visible, Yahweh is present, guiding the people (Ex 13:21-22), hiding them from the Egyptians (Ex 14:19, 24), entering into dialogue with Moses (when the cloud covers the Tent; Ex 33:9-10; Nm 12:5). When the people are to set out on their wilderness march, it is at the Lord's bidding, as signaled through the presence of the cloud (Nm 9:15-23).

Yahweh is a God present to and caring for Israel. This is, in fact, how the Bible explains the meaning of the name Yahweh (*Ehyeh asher Ehyeh*; Ex 3:14). Assisted by these very concrete signs, the failure of Israel's faith and their constant murmuring becomes all the more serious.

Blessing Recalled

As important as the theme of Israel's wandering and testing in the wilderness is, it is not the only theme in the book of Numbers. The deaths of Miriam (20:1) and of Aaron (20:22-29) are signs that the old generation is passing away. The people turn a corner, as it were, and begin to head north. Bypassing Edom (20:14-21) and Moab, and defeating Sihon, king of the Amorites, and Og, king of Bashan (21:10-35), they finally arrive at the plains of Moab, just across the Jordan River from Jericho (22:1). We are on the threshold between the wilderness period and entry into the land when Yahweh will fulfill the promises to the ancestors to bless them with a large family, with the presence of God, and with possession of the land. The last section of the book of Numbers looks to the future.

This comes into focus in the story of Balaam (22:2-24:25). Balaam was a renowned professional seer/prophet; an Aramaic text, dating from *ca.* 700 B.C., has been found in Deir 'Alla, a site in modern Jordan, which mentions him as a "seer of the gods." Balak, king of Moab, is afraid of Israel and summons Balaam repeatedly to come and utter curses against them. Solemn words of curse (or blessing; see Gen 27) were considered especially powerful.

But Balaam, though a pagan, speaks for Yahweh and is completely obedient to that "word of the Lord" (23:26). As Israel had finished its first round of murmuring and come to Sinai, we meet the pagan priest, Jethro (Ex 18), who responded to the mere story of Yahweh's doings with faith and worship. Now, after the second round of murmuring ends, as Israel arrives in the plains of Moab, we meet a pagan prophet who, ignoring the wishes of his "king-employer" and rejecting the offers of wealth and honor, is completely obedient to the word of Yahweh. Perhaps these pious pagans, priest and prophet, present a message and model of the kind of life (worship and obedience) that Israel was called to lead but so often failed to do.

When Balaam finally comes to Moab, despite some resistance from his donkey, he speaks four oracles, three of them requested by Barak, the final one offered "free." The content of all of them is essentially the same: Yahweh has and will continue to bless Israel. Allusions to the ancestral promise have crept up in the preceeding chapters (e.g., 11:12), but this is the first time since Genesis that the topic has been treated so extensively.

Israel is a unique people that "lives apart" and has become very numerous (23:9-10; see Gen 12:2; 13:16; 28:14). No harm can come to them because Yahweh, their king, is "with them" (23:21-23; see Gen 28:14-15; Ex 3:12-14). The third oracle speaks of the fulness of Yahweh's blessing which brings with it life, prosperity and power. Israel is like a well watered garden or like the mighty cedars (24:6-9; see Gen 12:2-3). Finally, Balaam describes Israel's coming victories over the surrounding peoples (24:14-25).

In these oracles, the promises of blessing stand out: numerous people, presence of God, and possession of the land (the peoples cannot resist Israel). Throughout all the wilderness period, Yahweh has been faithful to these promises, not because of, but in spite of Israel's behavior. The rest of the book of Numbers deals with further prescriptions for how Israel should behave after they enter the land.

Conclusion

Israel's time in the desert was a very important time. It is where they covenanted with Yahweh, and where they were tested in their faithfulness to that covenant. The desert is a place of extremes in which the basic questions are posed in clear and urgent ways. It is essentially a negative place, made positive only by the presence of God and the promise of what is to come. Will Israel be seduced by the idolatry of the past, preferring to return to Egypt, or will they recognize that their whole life is in the hands of Yahweh who cares for them and continues to be faithful to the promises?

"Remember how for forty years now the Lord, your God, has directed all your journeying in the desert, so as to test you by affliction and find out whether or not it was your intention to keep his commandments. He therefore let you be afflicted with hunger, and then fed you with manna . . . in order to show you that not by bread alone does one live but by every word that comes forth from the mouth of God" (Dt 8:2-3).

In the New Testament, Jesus will likewise undergo a "wilderness experience" just like Israel (Mt 4:1-11; Mk 1:12-13; Lk 4:1-13). The threefold temptation he faced there can actually be reduced to one: will he obediently accept and follow his calling by God in God's way, or will the seduction of false ways, of idols (e.g., power, possessions), lead him astray? Throughout these temptations, which characterized his whole ministry (Mt 16:23; Jn 6:14-15), Jesus was faithful. True life is found only in obedience to God.

Just as there are times when we are overwhelmed by chaos and we pray "out of the (watery) depths," so, too, we undergo our wilderness experiences. The religious questions and issues we face are basically the same as those we have seen in the Pentateuch and the New Testament. Do we want to stop our journey and stay where we are? Do we want to reverse it and live in the past? Will the legitimate concerns of food, drink, defense and stability become idols which govern our lives? Will we live our lives by the values which flow from our covenant with God? Will we be faithful to the God who calls us into new and unknown futures? We may not—in fact, usually we do not—know the details of the future, but that is all right. We do know the most important thing about it: we are not alone, and whatever the future may bring, we will make it together. The words addressed first to Israel speak to us as well, "Do not be afraid, for I am with you" (e.g., Gen 28:15; Ex 3:12; 14:13-14; Isa 41:10, 13).

✼

Suggested Readings

On Numbers in General:

B. Anderson, *UOT*, 110-22.
L. Boadt, *ROT*, 190-93.
R. Burns, *Exodus, Leviticus, Numbers* (OTM 3, 1983).
F. McCurley, *GELN*, 85-96.
H. Kenik Mainelli, *Numbers* (CBC 5, 1985).
C.L'Heureux, "Numbers," *NJBC* #5.

On the Symbolism of Forty:

R. Poelman, *Times of Grace: The Sign of Forty in the Bible* (New York: Herder and Herder, 1964).
M. Pope, "Number, Numbering, Numbers," *IDB* 3: 564-65.

On the Wilderness:

S. Talmon, "Wilderness," *IDBS*, 946-49.

On Place of Testing:

> B. Anderson, *UOT*, 113-16.
> L. Boadt, *ROT*, 191-93.
> F. McCurley, *GELN*, 91-96.

On Place of Presence:

> B. Anderson, *UOT*, 116-18.
> F. McCurley, *GELN*, 115-122.

On Balaam:

> B. Anderson, *UOT*, 121-22.
> A. Lemaire, "Fragments of the Book of Balaam found at Deir Alla," *BAR* 11:5 (Sept-Oct 1985) 27-39.

6

Deuteronomy: Hear, O Israel!

The Israelites have been encamped in the plains of Moab; it is now time to move on and enter the land. Before they do, however, Moses, in three discourses (1:1-4:43; 4:44-28:69; 29-30), reviews their history and reminds them of their covenant obligations. Their life and happiness in the land will depend on how seriously they are faithful to them. When this is completed, he dies and is buried in an unknown place (34:5-6). All of this comprises the book of Deuteronomy.

The name, Deuteronomy, deriving from two Greek words which mean "second law," is based on a mistaken translation of Dt 17:18. There it is said that the king should have a "copy of the law" to meditate on day and night. The Greek translated this, "this second law." The translator was influenced perhaps by the present arrangement of the Pentateuch where the "first law" is that found at Sinai (Ex 19-Nm 10); the "second law," which at times repeats material, especially from Ex 22-23, is that found collected here in Deuteronomy.

It would be misleading, however, to think of Deuteronomy simply as another law code. While the book does contain much legal material, this is found in the context of speeches. As the Israelites prepare to enter the land, Moses is urging and exhorting them to be faithful to their covenant; their life and future depend on it. Favorite expressions appear over and over again; motivations are often given in the laws to explain them and urge compliance. The tone is emotional and rhetorical. Because of this, some scholars have suggested that the background of Deuteronomy can be sought in the preaching of Levites at covenant renewal ceremonies, or in the preaching of earlier, northern prophets. Whatever the case may be, Deuteronomy is often described as "preached law."

Because of its great stress on the covenant and covenant loyalty, Deuteronomy has also been described as "the covenant document par excellence." We noted earlier, in our discussion of covenant, that many scholars see the Sinai covenant as reflecting, from the beginning, the model of a suzerainty treaty type of covenant. We preferred to follow those who see the Sinai covenant originally more as a family kinship covenant. When we come to Deuteronomy though, the parallels with the suzeraignty treaty, particularly of the Neo-Assyrian type, are much more pronounced. Similarities of structure and vocabulary abound. The reinterpretation of the covenant— from family kinship to suzerain-vassal—reflects a changed political and social reality in Israel. Whether this shift originated at the time of Deuteronomy or is more ancient is still being discussed. It is clear though that Deuteronomy reflects a much more consistent and thoroughgoing covenant theology.

Hear, O Israel

"These are the words which Moses spoke to all Israel . . ." (1:1). Moses speaks; Israel is repeatedly called on to hear, to listen (e.g., 5:1; 6:4; 9:1: 27:9). A favorite term for Israel is "the assembly of Yahweh," in Hebrew, the *qahal* of Yahweh (e.g., 5:19; 23:2-4, 9). The root *qahal*, probably related to the word *qol*, "voice," means "to assemble, call together." In the Greek, it is often translated as *ekklesia* which has a similar meaning and which is the source of the French and Spanish words for "church" (*église, iglesia*) and the English "ecclesiastic(al)." Israel then can almost be defined as "that community which hears the word of God (here spoken through Moses) and lives by that word" (4:33, 36; 5:24, 26; 8:3; Ex 20:19).

But there is more to this "hearing" than meets the eye (or the ear?). Moses exhorts Israel to hear/listen "with all your heart and all your soul" (e.g., 30:2; 11:13, 13:4). In the Bible, the primary organ of hearing is not the ear, though this is where the sound enters, but the heart. If the word goes in one ear and out the other, we have not truly "heard." When God offers to give Solomon whatever he requests, the king asks for "a listening heart" (1 Kgs 3:9). When we turn away our hearts, we do not listen (Dt 30:17). Likewise, if our heart is hardened or "uncircumcised," the word cannot enter and take effect (e.g., 10:16; 30:6; Ps 95:8; Jer 4:4).

In our popular understanding, the heart is the seat of emotions; in the Bible it is much more than that. The heart is the very center of the person. Often, its closest translation into English is "the mind." In the same way, "the soul" should not be confused with the spiritual part of the person as distinct from the material part. The "soul" (*nephesh*) is the whole, living, human person viewed, as it were, from the inside. To hear/ listen with the heart and soul means that we allow the word of God to enter deeply into our inner selves, to the very core of our persons; as a result, we are changed.

In the light of this, we can appreciate why the frequent expression, "to listen/hearken to the voice of God/the Lord"

(4:30; 30:2, 8, 10) is the Hebrew idiom for "to obey." In Greek (*hypakouein*) and Latin (*obaudire*) also, the words for "to obey" are compounds of the verb "to hear" (*akouein, audire*). If Israel truly hears, they will obey. Thus, in Deuteronomy, the call to Israel "to hear" is often closely joined with expressions like "and carefully observe" the commandments (e.g., 5:1; 6:3; 7:12, etc.). If Israel truly hears, the word of God will enter their hearts, will fill their minds, and their lives will be transformed. They will live as the covenant people that they are.

Remember, Do Not Forget

In addition to urging the people to hear, Moses frequently exhorts them to remember. "However, take care and be earnestly on your guard not to forget the things which your own eyes have seen, nor let them slip from your memory as long as you live, but teach them to your children and to your children's children" (4:9). See also, e.g., 4:23; 5:15; 6:12; 8:2, 11, 14, 18-19; 9:7, 27; 31:21.

They are to remember how Yahweh had led them out of Egypt (5:15; 6:12) and cared for them forty years in the wilderness (8:2), even though they had rebelled (9:7). They are not to forget Yahweh by worshipping other gods (8:19) or by neglecting the covenant commandments (8:11). Basically, they are called on to remember their story, the story of what God had done in Egypt, at the sea, in the wilderness, and of how they were to respond by their covenant-guided lives.

Memory is a very important, even an essential part of our lives. What is it that memory does? Not long ago, a news item told of a woman who appeared in the Midwest with no memory. She had complete amnesia. She did not know her name or who her family was; where she had come from, how she had gotten where she was, or where she was going. The article, with a picture, bore fruit; her family recognized her and brought her home.

Memory gives us identity; it gives us a home; it enables us to know who we are. By remembering Exodus-Sinai, Israel knew who they were: their whole lives, their whole existence were the gift of the redeemer God. They knew where they had come from and where they were going: Yahweh was leading them from Egypt into the future, fulfilling the promises to their ancestors. They also knew how they were to live, by faithfully observing the covenant.

Memory tells us, however, not only who we are, but also who we are not, or at least, not yet. The story of our God who wants us to be holy, "for I, the Lord your God, am holy" (Lev 19:2) also provides a vision by which we can recognize and measure our failures. The prophets will base their critiques of Israel on their common covenant memory. Memory will never let us settle down and say, "Let us stay here; we have done enough!" Memory of our past will push us on to live our lives more fully and more faithfully, ready to meet God coming toward us in the events of the future. As we noted above (p. 88), when we remember, we bring the past into the present in order to help us live in the future.

This aspect of memory appears in Deuteronomy in yet another way. Who is the Israel that Moses is addressing? It is not the Israel who had personally experienced Egypt, the Sea, Sinai, the early wanderings. That generation had died out. Moses is addressing a whole new Israel, and is telling them "to remember." It is obviously not a question of the original events. What they are to remember is the story, their story, and they are to pass this on to their children from generation to generation (4:9; 6:7, 20-25; 30:12-13).

The present generation does not need to go back into the past; in remembering, the events of the past are brought instead into the present. They become real again "today." And over and over again, Deuteronomy stresses the urgency of this "today."

> Hear, O Israel, the statutes and decrees which I proclaim in your hearing this day, that you may learn them and take care to observe them. The Lord, our God, made a covenant with us at Horeb; not with our fathers did he make this covenant, but with us, all of us who are alive here this day (5:1-3).

> This day the Lord, your God commands you to observe these statutes and decrees. Be careful then to observe them with all your heart and with all your soul. Today you are making this agreement with the Lord: he is to be your God and you are to walk in his ways and observe his statutes, commandments and decrees, and to hearken to his voice. And today the Lord is making this agreement with you . . . (26:16-18).

See also, 4:4, 20, 38, 40; 7:11; 8:1; 9:3; 11:8, 13, 32; 27:1, 4, 9-10, etc.

It is one of the functions of liturgy to make present the great events of the past so that each new generation can share in them and appropriate them for itself. Thus, Israel celebrates the Sabbath to remember God's creative activity (Ex 20:8-11) and also how they were redeemed from the slavery of Egypt (Dt 5:15). They celebrate Passover "that you may remember as long as you live the day of your departure from the land of Egypt" (Dt 16:3; see Ex 12:14). The Christian Eucharist is celebrated in fulfillment of Jesus' command. "Do this is memory of me" (Lk 22:19; 1 Cor 11:23-25). While it is

uncertain whether Deuteronomy itself has a liturgical background, the stress on memory can well direct us to this aspect
of our worship.

Israel is poised, ready to enter the land. It is crucial that they
remember and do not forget. A prolonged attack of amnesia
could prove fatal.

The Lord is Our God, the Lord Alone

"Hear, O Israel, the Lord is our God, the Lord alone" (6:4).
This is the beginning of the great prayer of Israel's faith, called,
after its first word in Hebrew, the *Shema'*. It is recited daily by
Jews up to the present. The most basic affirmation is that the
Lord, Yahweh, alone is God.

Yahweh is the God who brought Israel out of the land of
Egypt (5:6-7) with great signs and wonders. All of this was so
that they might know that "the Lord is God in the heavens
above and on the earth below, and there is no other" (4:34-35;
39). The recurring temptation for Israel was to worship other
gods; again, idolatry, not atheism, is the greatest sin against
covenant. Deuteronomy has very harsh things to say about
anyone, whether pagan nations, false prophets or even members of one's own family, who would lead Israel astray from its
basic faith in Yahweh (e.g., 7:1-5; 13:1-19). The urgency of
this cannot be overstated.

This great God of all the earth has become known to Israel
in and through its history. "Did anything so great ever happen
before? Was it ever heard of?" (4:32). Did any other god so
choose a nation for a special possession as Yahweh had in
leading Israel out of Egypt? (4:33-34). The Lord's great act
towards Israel was that of election. "For you are a people

sacred to the Lord, your God; he has chosen you from all the nations on the face of the earth to be a people peculiarly his own" (7:6; 14:2). Israel's special position is based on Yahweh's free choice.

But what could have prompted such a choice? Was it because Israel was a large and powerful nation? Large and powerful nations can be tempted to see themselves as deserving God's special favor. "It was not because you are the largest of all the nations that the Lord set his heart on you and chose you, for you are really the smallest of all nations" (7:4). Well, then, could it be because Israel was a righteous nation and deserved on its own merits to receive Yahweh's saving action? Self-righteous nations often see things in such a light. "Do not say to yourselves, 'It is because of my merits that the Lord has brought me in to possess this land' . . . it is not because of your own merits . . . for you are a stiff-necked people" (9:4-6).

God's election of Israel is not based on power or righteousness. It was simply "because the Lord loved you and because of his fidelity to the oath he had sworn to your fathers . . . " (7:8). And the promise to the ancestors was also based on love. "For love of your fathers he choose their descendents and personally led you out of Egypt . . . " (4:37). "Yet in his love for your fathers the Lord was so attached to them as to chose you, their descendents . . . " (10:15).

On occasion we hear the cliche, "The New Testament God is a God of love; the Old Testament God is a God of wrath and punishment." This is obviously false and does justice neither to the New nor the Old Testament. The New Testament knows wrath and punishment, just as the Old knows love. The whole unfolding of Israel's history with God is rooted in and flows out of God's prior love for Israel. This is expressed first in the promises to the ancestors and then in the deliverance of Israel from Egypt. It is the story of a God who first loved us. "The Lord is our God, the Lord alone" (6:4).

You Shall Love the Lord

How can Israel respond to such a gift? "Therefore, you shall love the Lord, your God, with all your heart, and with all your soul, and with all your strength" (6:5). "Therefore!" The only response to such love is love. Over and over again, Israel is called to just such a wholehearted loving response, a response which flows from the very center of their persons, and is manifested in their whole lives (e.g., 6:5; 10:12; 11:1; 13; 13:4).

The Lord's electing love and Israel's loving response find concrete expression in the covenant. The covenant, which embodies the interpersonal union between Yahweh and Israel, is not, as we have seen, just a reality from the past. It is now; it is "today" (26:16-19). Moses calls on the people to hear all the commandments and statutes and to observe them carefully. The commandments are not arbitrary laws, and their observance is not external compliance. Particular laws and statutes are concrete applications of the covenant life, and we observe them as expressions of our wholehearted, grateful response to God.

> "And now, Israel, what does the Lord, your God, ask of you but to fear the Lord, your God and follow his ways exactly, to love and serve the Lord, your God, with all your heart and all your soul, to keep the commandments and statutes of the Lord which I enjoin on you today for your own good?" (10:12-13).

We are a far cry here from any external legalism.

Because Israel is Yahweh's people and special possession, they are to worship only Yahweh. Repeatedly, as we have just noted, they are warned to beware of anyone or anything, either from within or without, which might lead them astray to follow other gods. When they enter the land, they must not make any covenant with the pagan nations, or intermarry with them, for they would "turn you from following me to serving other gods" (7:2-4). Rather, this is what they should do: "Tear down their altars, smash their sacred pillars, chop down their sacred poles, and destroy their idols by fire" (7:5; see also 7:16; 12:29-31).

The same seriousness applies to temptations which arise from within Israel. If anyone, prophet or dreamer, family member or friend, would lead you into idolatry, kill them (13:1-12)! The penalty is severe so that "all Israel, hearing of it, shall fear and never again do such evil as this in your midst" (13:12). Israel's whole life and existence depended on their fidelity to Yahweh and the covenant. To lead them astray from that fidelity constituted the gravest treason.

Israel must not only beware of foreign gods and their cults. They must also watch over their own worship to keep it pure and holy. The legislation in Deuteronomy makes it clear that Israel's worship should be centered in that place which Yahweh chooses, where Yahweh's name dwells, most likely a reference to Jerusalem. Whether it is a question of holocausts (12:14), votive offerings (12:26), tithes (14:23), the Passover (16:5-6), or the offering of first fruits (26:1-11), they should be celebrated at that place. And their celebrations should be joyful! In all these rituals, Israel is told to rejoice, to make merry before the Lord (12:7, 12, 18; 14:26; 16:11, 14; 26:11; 27:7).

Because Israel is Yahweh's people, how they treat others is also of critical importance, so many of the laws of Deuteronomy touch on diverse areas of social life. Living the covenant means being concerned about the welfare of the poor (15:1-18; 23:19-20; 24:14-15, 19-22). It means practicing justice in the legal system (16:18-20; 19:15-21; 24:17-18) as well as in the economic sphere (25:13-16). It means caring about the natural environment (20:19-20; 22:6-7; 25:4).

Deuteronomy is concerned with the establishment of a society which will reflect the justice and mercy of God. To this end, it sets out, as it were, a constitution for Israel's life as God's people. The leadership of the community is vested in king, priest and prophet, but each of these has limitations (17:14-18:22). The judiciary is set up (16:18-20; 17:8-13) and is admonished that "justice and justice alone shall be your aim" (16:20). Individual laws and cases show Israel's respect for the sacredness of life and the worth of individual personhood. Each member of the community, regardless of sex, age or class should be treated with respect (19:1-25:19). Israel may have left Egypt as a "mixed rabble" (Ex 12:38; Nm 11:4), but when they enter the land, they are to be an organized society concerned for the rights of all.

Israel is to respond to Yahweh with a wholehearted love. But what does it mean to love the Lord? As one writer has recently expressed it, "Love in Deuteronomy is always a verb, an action, never simply an inner emotion. God's love toward Israel consisted in his deliverance of her out of Egypt, his guidance of her through the wilderness, and his gift to her of the promised land (cf., 26:5-9). So, too, Israel's love toward God was to be active obedience in response to his love. But what is the content of that obedience? Concretely, what does God command? All the laws in Deuteronomy are intended to spell out the answer. They are explications of what it means to love God" (E. Achtemeier, *Int* 41: 278-79).

Covenant Blessing and Covenant Curse

Moses urges Israel to covenant fidelity as if their very life depended on it—and it did. Covenant blessing follows on covenant fidelity, and covenant curse follows on covenant infidelity. This was a common element in ancient Near Eastern covenant making, and many of the treaty covenants which have been preserved contain long lists of blessings and curses, which the patron gods of the respective parties are supposed to oversee. As part of his exhortation, Moses frequently appeals to such blessings and curses (4:25-28; 6:14-15; 7:12-26; 8:19-20; 11:10-17, 22-32; 28:1-68; 29:21-28; 30:15-20).

"I set before you here, this day, a blessing and a curse: a blessing for obeying the commandments of the Lord, your God, which I enjoin on you today . . . " (11:26-27). Blessing is, as we have often noted before, the power of life, and it is manifested first in the gift of the land (5:32-33; 6:18; 8:1, 7-9). Abraham, Isaac and Jacob and their descendents had been promised a land; God is about to fulfill that promise. And it is a good land with natural water and abundant crops (8:7-9). In addition, God will send the rain to produce grain, wine and oil so there will be plenty of food (11:10-15). Their flocks and herds will also know abundant fertility (7:12-15).

The Israelites themselves will have long life in the land (e.g., 5:33). They will not know sickness or disease (7:15); nor will anyone among them be childless (7:13-14). They will dwell in security and have nothing to fear from enemies without, because the Lord is in their midst (7:16-26; 11:22-25). All of the covenant blessings are conveniently summarized in chapter 28:1-14.

" . . . a curse, if you do not obey the commandments of the

Lord, your God, but turn aside from the way I ordain for you today, to follow other gods whom you have not known" (11:28). Curse is the power of death, and the covenant curses are basically the reverse of the blessings just described.

As a punishment for disobedience, especially following strange gods, the land will be dry and barren, like sulphur and salt (29:21-28) or iron (28:23-24). There will be no rain; the sky will be like bronze over their heads (28:23-24; 11:16-17). The soil will produce no crops; the people will perish from lack of food (11:17). They will know sickness, pestilence, wasting and fever (28:20-22); they will not live in the land for any length of time (4:25-28). Nations will invade and besiege them (28:49-58); they will lose everything—wife, children, house, animals, produce of the soil (28:29b-35). They will be scattered abroad among their enemies (28:63-68; 4:28). In other words, the wrath of Yahweh will flare up and destroy them from the face of the land (6:14-15). Again, chapter 28:15-68 offers a summary, at times with lurid details, of the covenant curses on covenant infidelity.

The covenant blessings and curses serve as good reminders to us, who tend at times to overspiritualize our lives, of how firmly enmeshed we truly are, both with the natural world and with other people. They remind us also, once again, that the only path to life lies in fidelity, slavery, to Yahweh. And, as always, idolatry, following false gods, leads only to death and doom (30:15). Moses' words to Israel are a good summary of covenant morality:

> I have set before you life and death, the blessing and the curse. Choose life, then, that you and your descendents may live by loving the Lord, your God, heeding his voice, and holding fast to him. For that will mean life for you, a long life for you to live on the land which the Lord swore he would give your fathers Abraham, Isaac and Jacob (30:19b-20).

The Death of Moses, Servant of God

"The Lord said to Moses, 'The time is now approaching for you to die . . . '" (31:14). Joshua is appointed to lead the people into the land (31:23), though it is made very clear that it is, in fact, Yahweh who goes before them to give the land (31:3, 8). Moses then hands on two songs to the whole assembly; one is a song of judgment and warning (32:1-43); the other, one of blessing on the tribes (33:1-29). Going up Mt. Nebo, he gazes out across the Jordan at the promised land, a land he may not enter, and dies (34:1-5). He was buried there in Moab, but no one knows where (34:6).

God is, of course, the dominant actor in the Pentateuch, but among human figures, Moses is clearly the most important. From his birth at the beginning of Exodus, which foreshadows Israel's later deliverance, to his death at the end of Deuteronomy, Moses' whole life is tied up with Israel and God's acts on behalf of that people. It is in and through Moses that God most often speaks and acts.

Moses is the leader of the people, at times attaining heroic dimensions. In the confrontation with Pharaoh, he speaks God's message, and when this is resisted, he performs signs and wonders often using his "staff-of-God," which functions almost like a magic wand. It turns into a snake and back again (Ex 7:8-13); it turns the Nile into blood (Ex 7:17, 20) and produces the frogs (Ex 8:1); at its touch, the dust becomes gnats (Ex 8:12-13). It splits the sea in two (Ex 14:16), and brings water from the rock (Nm 20:8, 11).

More important than his doing dramatic deeds is Moses' role as a prophet. Deuteronomy, in fact, considers him the greatest of all the prophets (34:10-12). A prophet in the Bible is not primarily someone who foretells the future, as in our popular English usage. A prophet is rather someone who is called to speak for God. This is made quite clear in Dt 18:17, "I will put my words into his mouth; he shall tell them all that I command him" (see also Ex 7:1-2).

Moses' call at the burning bush (Ex 3-4) shows striking

similarities to the call of a prophet. Like Jeremiah (Jer 1:4-8), he is called to bring a message which will not be well received; he registers objections why he should not be the one to do this; God turns these aside with the assurance that "I will be with you" (Ex 3:12; Jer 1:8). And like a prophet confronting the kings and leaders, Moses goes to Pharaoh.

Moses brings God's word not only to the Egyptians, but also to the Israelites. At Sinai, Moses speaks with God on the mountain (e.g., Ex 19:3-14, 19, 20-25; Dt 5:22-31) and mediates to the people the covenant law. God gives the Israelites their Torah through Moses. In the great speeches of Deuteronomy, Moses teaches the law to the people (4:5, 14; 5:31; 6:1), challenging them to covenant fidelity and rebuking them for their failures. God's voice and Moses' voice often blend together. Corresponding to Moses who speaks God's word is Israel, the *qahal* that listens, that hears.

Unfortunately, the people do not always listen. They also murmur and rebel. When this happens, Moses exercises another prophetic function. As an intermediary, the prophet speaks to the people on behalf of God; but at times, the prophet must speak to God on behalf of the people. The prophet is also an intercessor (see, e.g., Am 7:1-6; Jer 7:16; 21:1-10). Moses intercedes for the people after the golden calf incident (Ex 32-34; Dt 9:7-29; 10:10-11) and frequently during the wilderness murmuring (e.g., Nm 14:10b-20).

And yet, this prophet, teacher, intercessor, leader, wonder-worker, perhaps the greatest figure in Israel's history, died before entering the promised land! How could this be explained? There was only one possible explanation: Moses was being punished for sin. The only question was: Was he being punished for some sin of his own, or for the sins of others? Both answers appear in the Pentateuch.

During the wandering in the wilderness, the community came to Kadesh where the people grumbled because they had no water (Nm 20:2-13). God tells Moses to take his staff and bring water from the rock. After assembling the people, he rebukes them, "Listen to me, you rebels! Are we to bring water for you from this rock?" Then he struck the rock twice, and water came forth. "But the Lord said to Moses and Aaron, 'Because you were not faithful to me in showing forth my sanctity before the Israelites, you shall not lead this community into the land I will give them'" (Nm 20:12; see also Dt 32:48-52).

That Moses is being punished is clear; exactly what the sin is, is not. Faced with this obscurity, scholars have proposed various solutions. For some, the gift of water was a sign of God's compassion; by rebuking the people, Moses distorted the meaning of the gift. For others, Moses struck the rock twice because he lacked sufficient faith to do it with one blow. All these suggestions, as well as others, are somewhat speculative; it almost seems as if our present text has deliberately obscured the sin while leaving the basic point intact.

Deuteronomy offers the other solution. "The Lord was angered against me also on your account, and said, 'Not even you shall enter there . . . '" (Dt 1:37; 3:23-28; 4:21-22). Moses was the Lord's faithful servant (Dt 3:24; 34:5), but he was not allowed to enter the land because of the sins of the people. He suffered on their account. In this, Moses is very like another prophet, the suffering servant of Isa 53:4-5, "Yet, it was our infirmities he bore, our sufferings he endured . . . (he was) crushed for our sins."

"So there in the land of Moab, Moses, the servant of the Lord died as the Lord had said; and he was buried in the ravine opposite Beth-peor in the land of Moab, but to this day no one knows the place of his burial" (Dt 34:5-6).

Conclusion

Encamped in the plains of Moab, Israel is suspended in space and time; they are between Egypt, Sinai and the past, on the one hand, and Canaan and the future, on the other. They are on the threshold of a new life. If they are to have a future with a full life, they must be faithful to their covenant with Yahweh. Moses urgently and eloquently exhorts them to that fidelity. The one God, out of love, has chosen this one people as a special possession; they, also out of love, are to respond wholeheartedly through their one worship and their obedience to the one Torah.

The spirituality of Deuteronomy is deep, rich, and challenging. It also contains some dangers, two of which are worth noting here. First, the stress on "covenant fidelity leads to covenant blessing" (a primary principle in the interpretation of Israel's history in the following books of Joshua, Judges, Samuel, and Kings, the so-called Deuteronomic History), if applied mechanically, can become simplistic. It can lead to a "success-oriented" spirituality with its concomitant bargaining with God. "If I am obedient and do X or Y, God will come through with the blessings." Our experience, as well as that within the Old Testament as a whole, knows that things do not always work out this way. The whole question of the suffering of the innocent (i.e., covenant fidelity is followed by curse!) gives expression to this realization. The ways of God with humanity are much more mysterious than any simplistic formula.

Secondly, Deuteronomy exposes one of the weaknesses of the Mosaic covenant spirituality: sectarianism. "We are saved, and you are not!" Within the covenant community, a high morality is in evidence, but this does not extend too far outside. Other peoples are seen primarily as threats to Israel's faith and are to be dealt with accordingly. Again, within the Old Testament as a whole, a more universal attitude appears; we have seen it already in the book of Genesis, in the primeval history, and in the promises to the ancestors (to which Deuteronomy itself alludes, e.g., 7:8; 10:15). That these pitfalls are real can be illustrated easily from many of our popular radio and TV preachers.

As we reach the end of Deuteronomy, we realize that these urgent words of Moses to the people are, in fact, his last words. And as Moses' life comes to an end, so does Deuteronomy and the whole Torah. The people, in a real way, no longer need Moses. From now on, they will be led by the living word of the Torah. Phrased differently, Moses may be dead and buried (and who knows where?), but he continues to live and do his work; he leads and guides the people; he communicates God's will to them; he challenges them to covenant fidelity in and through the Torah, God's word in the midst of the people. This will go with them as they journey across the Jordan and into the promised land; it will be handed on to the next generation, and the generation after that, down through the ages, even to the present time (Dt 4:9; 6:7, 20-25; 31:12-13).

Suggested Readings

On Deuteronomy in General:

E. Achtemeier, *Deuteronomy, Jeremiah* (Proclamation Commentaries; Philadelphia: Fortress Press, 1978) 9-47.

B. Anderson, UOT, 376-88.

J. Blenkinsopp, "Deuteronomy," NJBC #6.

L. Boadt, ROT, 193; 347-56.

R. Clifford, *Deuteronomy* (OTM 4, 1982).

L. Hoppe, *Deuteronomy* (CBC 6, 1985).

N. Lohfink, "Deuteronomy," *IDBS*, 229-32.

R. Murphy, "Deuteronomy: A Document of Revival," Spiritual Revivals (Concilium 89; New York: Herder & Herder, 1973) 26-36.

The whole issue of *Int* 41:3 (July 1987) is devoted to Deuteronomy and contains the following four articles:

S.D. McBride, Jr., "Polity of the Covenant People," pp. 229-44.

P. Miller, "Moses My Servant," pp. 245-55.

J.G. Janzen, "The Yoke that Gives Rest," pp. 256-68.

E. Achtemeier, "Plumbing the Depths," pp. 269-81.

On the Old Testament Understanding of "Heart" and "Soul":

H.W. Wolff, *Anthropology of the Old Testament* (Philadelphia: Fortress Press, 1974) 40-58, 10-25.

On Deuteronomy as a Constitution for Israel:

S.D. McBride, "Polity of the Covenant People," *Int* 41 (1987) 229-44.

On Deuteronomy and the Love Response:

E. Achtemeier, "Plumbing the Depths," *Int* 41 (1987) 269-81.

On the Death of Moses:

P. Miller, "Moses My Servant," *Int* 41 (1987) 245-55.

7

The Pentateuch: Mythos and Ethos

The Pentateuch was the first part of the Old Testament to be canonized. "Canon" means "norm, or guide," and it was in the early postexilic period that the group of priests who had come to fill the leadership vacuum left by the ending of the monarchy established these writings as the guide and norm for the continued existence of the Jewish community. Here they would find their identity, the root and source of their lives and their spirituality.

While the Pentateuch does contain historical memories, this is not its primary function as canonical literature. As one writer has expressed it, "It is not primarily a source book for the history of Israel . . . but rather a mirror for the identity of the believing community which in any era turns to it to ask who it is and what it is to do, even today" (J.A. Sanders, TC, xv-xvi). In the Torah we see a reflection of ourselves and our God.

Having worked our way through the Pentateuch, it may be helpful now, at the end, to offer something by way of summary and review. We will mention two suggestions in this regard before building on and expanding a third. These should not be viewed as mutually exclusive, as if only one of them is "the correct view"; they are, rather, different perspectives on the one unity of the Pentateuch.

Four Themes

One scholar (Roland de Vaux) has proposed that the religious meaning of the Pentateuch can be synthesized around four themes: promise, election, covenant, and law. Each of the stories of the primeval history ends on a note of hope and *promise*, climaxing in the promise to Abraham. The call of Abraham is also an act of *election*, a choosing by God which comes to its fullest expression in the call/election of the people, Israel. This election finds embodiment in the concrete relationship of the *covenant*, "I will be your God: you will be my people." Israel shows its fidelity to this covenant relation in and through its obedience to the covenant *law*. These are "the golden threads which weave in and out in the course of the Pentateuch."

One Theme: Promise of Blessing

Another scholar (David J.A. Clines), in an extended literary study, has proposed that the theme of the Pentateuch is *"the partial fulfillment—which implies also the partial non-fulfillment of the promise to or blessing of the patriarchs. The promise or blessing is both the divine initiative in a world where human initiatives always lead to disaster, and a re-affirmation of the primal divine intention for man.* The promise has three elements: posterity, divine-human relationship, and land. The posterity-element of the promise is dominant in Genesis 12-50, the relationship-element in Exodus and Leviticus, and the land-element in Numbers and Deuteronomy" (emphasis in the original, TP, 29). The primal history in Genesis 1-11 sets the stage and explains why the earth is in need of the promise of blessing.

This proposal might be schematized like this:

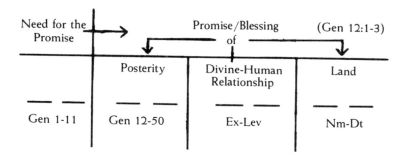

We have, in fact, noted these elements at various places in our study of the Pentateuch.

Mythos and Ethos

Our third, and last, proposal (based on work by James A. Sanders) sees the Torah as a combination of *mythos* and *ethos*. "In a canonical perspective, the Torah is a balanced inter-mingling of story and law: they go together; they belong together; and Torah means both. . . . Torah never lost or loses the *mythos-ethos* dual character" (J.A. Sanders, *FSSTST*, 43).

Our English terms, "myth" and "ethics," come to us weighted down, as it were, in our popular usage with certain unhelpful connotations. Thus, "myth" is often used to refer to something which is not true (e.g., "it is only a myth"). The term "ethics" at times conjures up ideas of detached, abstract obligations. Because of this, we prefer to retain the Greek forms *mythos* and *ethos* so that it will be clear that we are using these in a special and technical sense.

What do we understand by these terms? *Mythos* refers to the narrative or story which a given community shares and in which it finds its coherent view of the world: How do all the parts fit together? How do I/we find meaning within it? It is the "big story" of God and the cosmos within which the "small story" of my/our life is located and out of which I/we live. *Mythos* encompasses our deepest and truest understandings of all that is.

Ethos refers to my/our role within that story. How am I/we to live, to relate, to behave so that I/we can be free, happy, and responsible within this world? In addition to obligations, *ethos* includes a whole atmosphere of values, ideals and aspirations. At times we may stress *mythos*, at other times, *ethos*, but the two are closely interrelated. The Torah embraces both.

When the Torah people, as a community, tells its story, its *mythos*, the primary focus is on God. God is the creator of the universe who calls all things into existence. Human beings, men and women, are created in God's image to continue the creative activity of subduing chaos and giving life. They fail to do this and instead of life and order they beget death and brokenness. God's will for life and blessing, however, will not be ultimately frustrated, so God begins to choose a people to prepare them to live as true images, responding in faith and working to make things whole. When this people is oppressed in Egypt, God frees them from slavery and injustice and leads them, through Moses, to Sinai where they enter into covenant. Then, throughout their years in the wilderness, this God is present to them, bringing life and strength.

Throughout the *mythos*, God is a God who overcomes

chaos and brokenness: in creating a world from primordial chaos; in freeing from the chaos (the Sea) of slavery in Egypt; in guiding and nourishing through the chaos of wilderness and death. In place of chaos, God gifts this people, all peoples, the whole universe, with life, peace and wholeness. Even though the story may be told in the past tense, it is appropriate also to use verbs in the present tense. Chaos, death, brokenness, oppression, injustice, wilderness are present realities, too, and what God has done in the past, God continues to do in the present. This is what God is like in the Torah story.

The Torah presents us also with a vision of what we, as humans, are called to be, of how we are to live. It presents us with an *ethos* and a morality. Too often in the past, Old Testament covenant morality has been caricatured by Christians as an extrinsic legalism or minimalism. It is true that the Torah can be approached in that way, and at times this has happened. In the same way, the Gospel of Jesus can be, and has been, reduced to such a legalism. It is also true, however, that the Torah itself, and likewise the Gospel, calls for a rather different kind of response.

The *ethos* presented to us in the Torah can be described as one of *response* and one of *dialogue*. In the first instance, we *respond*. We respond to all the good gifts of creation, redemption and blessing that we have received from God. In the Torah, as we have seen, this response is specified in various ways: we are to serve, worship only Yahweh; we are to listen to (i.e., to obey) the word of God; we are to fear the Lord, our God (e.g., Dt 10:12; 6:13, etc.). "Fear of the Lord" in the Old Testament should not be viewed primarily as a feeling or emotion. It is used most often to refer to the humble, religious response of the whole person before the awesome God.

We are to serve, obey, fear the Lord; the Lord does not

serve, obey and fear us! The *ethos* of the Torah, however, is also one of *dialogue*. Just as God has loved us, so are we to love God and each other. Just as God subdued chaos and blessed us with life, so are we to share dominion and be life-giving. Just as God frees from oppression and injustice, so are we to be marked by our concern and efforts to put an end to these conditions. Just as God is faithful to the covenant, so are we to be faithful. If we fail to do these things, to that extent, despite what we may say, we are not serving, hearing, or fearing this God. God is present to and continues to act in our world in and through our God-like actions. That is why it is so important that we first hear and then remember the story, the *mythos* of our God.

In the course of our study, we have seen that, in the Torah, our role as humans is presented in two ways. In the context of creation, we are called to be images of God; in the context of redemption from Egypt, we are called to be slaves of Yahweh. Both of these reflect the twofold *ethos* of response and dialogue. To be image is to recognize and accept this fact: Each of us is the gift of, and dependent on the creative word of God. To be slave is to recognize and accept this fact: being freed from slavery to Pharaoh, we owe our worship, our service to Yahweh alone. To be an image is to be life-giving, peace-making, and justice-doing in the image of God. To be a slave is to manifest our service of Yahweh by taking our social relationships seriously and therefore not becoming oppressors in turn. Being a slave of Yahweh points the way and helps us to live out our call to imagehood. The *ethos* of the Torah is one of response and one of dialogue.

The individual commands and laws of the Torah are not meant to be exhaustive. They are, rather, individual, concrete examples of how we are to live the covenant. They are part of and serve a higher, more encompassing vision. In other words, what is the goal of all this? Where is it heading? What does the Torah, *mythos* and *ethos*, lead us to? Or, what is God's purpose and intention for us and for all of creation?

The goal of the Torah can be summed up in three words which we have met often in our study: life, peace, justice. All of these terms are, above all, terms of relationship, and they cover all the relationships of our lives: to God, to the natural world, to others, and to ourselves. These concerns emerge in the first verses of Genesis and run throughout the Torah, and in fact, throughout the whole Bible. God is a God of life, wholeness, peace and justice who desires the same for creation. Too often, by rejecting our role (as image and as slave), we bring about death, brokenness, injustice and the collapse of peace. The Torah warns us of this and deals with our recurring temptations. Thus, Adam and Eve; Cain and Abel; Abraham and Sarah; Joseph and his brothers; the Israelites oppressed in Egypt; the Israelites murmuring in the wilderness; these are all us, reflections of ourselves and our problems. The Torah also sets out to show us how to live otherwise so that God's will may be done on earth as it is in heaven. The purpose of the Torah, of the Pentateuch, is summed up concisely in a text we noted above, Dt 30:19:

> I have set before you life and death, the blessing and the curse,
> Choose life . . . .

Torah: Revelation

At the very beginning of our study, in chapter one, we saw that the Pentateuch is often called "the Law of Moses." Thus, the Hebrew word, *torah*, is translated "law." Then, with the help of some New Testament arguments, a radical contrast is drawn between "the Law," on the one hand, and "the Gospel," on the other. While this may be an attempt to deal with a religious problem, as real in Christianity as in Judaism, unfortunately it seriously misrepresents the nature of Torah, which, as we have just seen, includes both gospel and law, *mythos* and *ethos.*

A much better term than "law" to help us grasp what Torah is all about would be "revelation." In the Torah, we find the revelation of God to the people; it tells us who God is, and what God is up to in our world. In the light of these insights, we see who we are, and how we are to live. "In the broadest sense, (Torah) designates the divine will for Israel in the covenant relationship—both specific directive and the entire body of tradition that relates God's gracious acts and anticipates Israel's obedient response . . . . It thus includes the whole of revelation preserved in writing or orally—all that God has made known of his character, purpose and expectation" (J.A. Sanders, *FSSTST*, 111).

Since Christians find the fulness of revelation in Jesus Christ, we can see that Torah functions within Judaism in the same way that Jesus does within Christianity. Realizing this, perhaps we can appreciate more the Torah psalms (1, 19, 119).

Jesus: Fulfillment of the Torah

"Do not think that I have come to abolish the law and the prophets. I have come, not to abolish them, but to fulfill them" (Mt 5:17). Jesus here presents himself as the fulfillment of the Torah, so it becomes very important for Christians to know exactly what Torah means. This is exactly what we have been trying to do. It is not a question merely of finding a particular verse here and there in the Torah which can then be applied to Christ. In a real sense, Jesus fulfills the whole Torah. The Torah, *mythos* and *ethos*, is not replaced. Rather, for Christians, its light, which is already quite powerful, must be seen refracted further through the prism of the person, the life and teachings of Jesus.

Jesus embodies the revelation of God; the story of Jesus is our *mythos*. All things were created through him (e.g., Jn 1:3; Col 1:16); and it is through him that our redemption from the slavery of sin and death is accomplished (e.g., Rom 5:8-10; Heb 2:14-15). He is present with us on our journey all days, even to the end of the world (Mt 28:20).

As truly human, Jesus also embodies the full response to God; the story of Jesus is also our *ethos*. He passes through the water (here, of the Jordan) and is led into the wilderness where he undergoes the same basic temptations against covenant that Israel did. His replies to these temptations are all quotations taken from the Torah (e.g., Mt 3:13-4:11; see Dt 8:3; 6:16, 13). He is completely faithful to the will of God, and preaches the coming of God's kingdom of peace, justice, and love. His life, example, and teaching are the commandments of the new covenant (e.g., Jn 15:12).

Since in him the divine and the human are indissolubly bound together, Jesus, in his person, is the new covenant, sealed with a meal and a blood ritual (e.g., Mt 26:26-29). He also embodies the goal of the covenant: he is life (Jn 11:25); he is justice (1 Cor 1:30); he is peace in whom all things are made whole (Eph 2:11-22).

In chapter two, we noted that at the beginning of any spirituality lies some conception of God and the human and of their interrelationship. All subsequent beliefs and practices are based on and derive from these. We then began our study of the Pentateuch by reflecting on the first chapter of Genesis with its challenge that we live as images of God. We can now conclude our study by citing another text, one which in many ways depends on and speaks out of the perspective set forth in Genesis:

> He is the image of the invisible God,
> the first-born of all creatures.
> In him everything in heaven and
> on earth was created . . . all were created
> through him, and for him.
> He is before all that is.
> In him everything continues in being.
> It is he who is head of the body, the church;
> he who is the beginning
> the first-born of the dead,
> so that primacy may be his in everything.
> It pleased God to make absolute fulness
> reside in him and by means of him
> to reconcile everything in his person,
> both on earth and in the heavens,
> making peace
> through the blood of his cross (Col 1:15-20).

How can we truly understand what this means and how we are to live it without some knowledge of and appreciation for that part of the Old Testament that we call the Pentateuch, the Torah?

DIVINE AND HUMAN IN THE PENTATEUCH

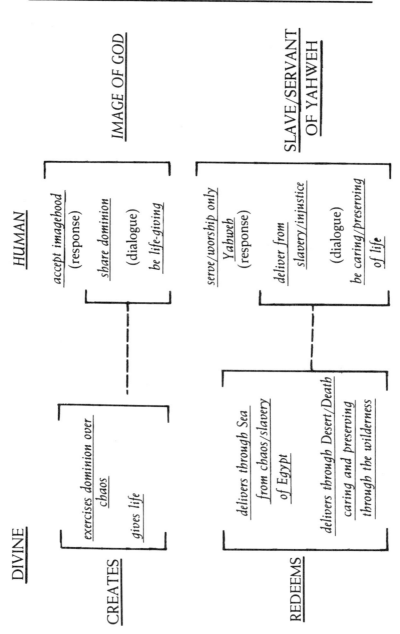

꒰

Suggested Readings

The Four Themes of R. deVaux:

This appeared originally in French in deVaux's introduction to the Pentateuch and Genesis for the Jerusalem Bible. This can be found now in:

The New Jerusalem Bible (Garden City, NY; Doubleday, 1985) 14-16.

Mythos and Ethos:

The work of James Sanders can be found in two books:
Torah and Canon (Philadelphia: Fortress Press, 1972) =TC
From Sacred Story to Sacred Text (Philadelphia: Fortress Press, 1987) = FSSTST. This is a collection of articles published previously over a period of years. Particularly helpful are:
"Torah and Christ," pp. 41-60 (= *Int* 29 (1975) 372-90).
"Torah: A Definition," pp. 111-14 (= *IDBS*, 909-11).

Abbreviations

BAR   *Bibli cal Archeology Review*

CBC   *Collegeville Bible Commentary* (Collegeville, MN: Liturgical Press).

CBQ   *Catholic Biblical Quarterly*

FSSTST   *From Sacred Story to Sacred Text* by James A. Sanders (Philadelphia: Fortress Press, 1987).

GELN   *Genesis, Exodus, Leviticus, Numbers* by Foster McCurley (Proclamation Commentaries; Philadelphia: Fortress Press, 1979).

IDB   *Interpreter's Dictionary of the Bible* 4 vols. (Nashville: Abingdon, 1962).

IDBS   *Interpreter's Dictionary of the Bible, Supplementary Volume* (Nashville: Abingdon, 1976).

Int   *Interpretation*

NJBC   *Jerome Biblical Commentary*, ed. Raymond E. Brown, Joseph A. Fitzmyer, and Roland E. Murphy (Englewood Cliffs, NJ: Prentice-Hall, 1990).

JSOT   *Journal for the Study of the Old Testament*

OTM   *Old Testament Message* (Wilmington, DE: Michael Glazier).

ROT   *Reading the Old Testament* by Lawrence Boadt (Ramsey, NJ: Paulist Press, 1984).

TC   *Torah and Canon* by James A. Sanders (Philadelphia: Fortress Press, 1972).

TD   *Theology Digest*

TP   *The Theme of the Pentateuch* by David J.A. Clines
                (Sheffield, England: JSOT Press, 1978).

UOT   *Understanding the Old Testament* by Bernhard Anderson
                (4th edition; Englewood Cliffs, NJ: Prentice-Hall,
                1986).

Biblical Index
Excluding the Pentateuch
Old Testament

New Testament

SUBJECT INDEX